Discovering
ALABAMA
WETLANDS

THE UNIVERSITY OF ALABAMA PRESS   TUSCALOOSA AND LONDON

Discovering
ALABAMA
WETLANDS

TEXT BY DOUG PHILLIPS

PHOTOGRAPHS BY ROBERT P. FALLS SR.

FOREWORD BY EDWARD O. WILSON

Copyright © 2002
The University of Alabama Press
Tuscaloosa, Alabama 35487-0380
All rights reserved
Printed in Korea by Pacifica Communications

Designer: Michele Myatt Quinn
Typeface: Granjon

∞

The paper on which this book is printed meets the minimum
requirements of American National Standard for Information
Science-Permanence of Paper for Printed Library Materials,
ANSI Z39.48-1984.

Publication of this volume was made possible in part by grants from
the Nature Conservancy of Alabama and the Robert G. Wehle
Charitable Trust.

Library of Congress Cataloging-in-Publication Data

Phillips, Douglas Jay.
   Discovering Alabama wetlands / text by Doug Phillips ; photo-
graphs by Robert P. Falls Sr. ; foreword by Edward O. Wilson.
       p.   cm.
   Includes bibliographical references (p. 103).
   ISBN 0-8173-1171-8 (cloth : alk. paper)
   1. Wetlands—Alabama. 2. Wetland ecology—Alabama. I. Title.
QH105.A2 P48 2002
578.768'09761—dc21   2002003113

British Library Cataloguing-in-Publication Data available

CONTENTS

Great blue heron (*Ardea herodias*) silently eyeing its next meal, Gulf State Park.

FOREWORD

From the cool temperate forests of the southernmost Appalachian highlands to the barrier islands of the Gulf of Mexico, Alabama's wild habitats are among the most diverse in the United States. The large fauna and flora they harbor also rank among the least explored and heralded. Alabama's citizens have only begun to awaken to the fullness of this heritage, and to assign it value in proportionate degree.

Alabama is (if I may be allowed to coin a term) the Aquatic State. It deserves that title from the exuberance of life in its freshwater and wetland environments. The number of fish and mollusk species is quite enormous, possibly setting a record not just for the United States but for the entire North Temperate Zone of the planet. Riverine swamps, marshes and bogs, and springheads that abound throughout the state harbor many unique animals and plants. A rich biota and the abundant clean fresh water that supports them are to be counted among the blessings of Alabama. As natural history and field biology increase in popularity, the natural heritage of the state is certain to rise in esteem both within the state and elsewhere.

As Robert Falls and Doug Phillips show in this volume with an account born of long experience, the wetlands of Alabama are not just biologically diverse but exquisitely beautiful. In different places and ways, they are variously mysterious, astonishing, and spiritual. In an aesthetic sense, and not just economically and scientifically, they contribute immeasurably to the quality of life in Alabama.

As a young naturalist growing up in Alabama in the 1940s, adventurous and open to new experiences as only a child can be, I had the great good fortune of exploring at leisure the kinds of wetlands depicted by Falls and Phillips. Biking back and forth along the causeway that borders the southern edge of the Mobile–Tensaw Delta (Alabama's equivalent of the Everglades), trekking across swamps and pitcher-plant meadows, and exploring marshes along the Gulf beaches and streams that feed the Tennessee River, I was imprinted permanently to the life of a naturalist and ecologist.

I set out during those formative years to learn all of the fifty or so snake species, a record-size fauna for North America, and succeeded, then turned to frogs

The endangered wood stork (*Mycteria americana*) is usually found in coastal areas.

and salamanders, among the most diverse on the continent. Given access to collections of the Tennessee Valley Authority, I also tried to learn the freshwater fishes. This time I failed. I didn't realize that Alabama is home to approximately 310 species, of which at least 28 percent were still unknown to science.

I am thankful that most of the places I knew as a boy and subsequently as a student at the University of Alabama still exist. But, as Falls and Phillips document, they are also very much at risk. Pressed by a growing population and soaring economic development, the 7.5 million acres of wetlands present before European settlement have been cut to 3.5 million acres. Almost all of the old-growth bottomland forests have been clear-cut, and most of the rivers impounded. According to the Association for Biological Information (now NatureServe), an affiliate of The Nature Conservancy, Alabama ranks with California and Hawaii as one of the states with the most species endangerment and extinction. By far the greatest loss has occurred in its aquatic environments. *Discovering Alabama Wetlands* contains much good news about the natural history of Alabama, worthy of celebration, but with it a warning that calls for wisdom and prudence on the behalf of future generations.

EDWARD O. WILSON
Professor Emeritus, Harvard University, and
Member, Alabama Academy of Honor

Wetland with wildflowers in bloom, countering the myth that such areas are unappealing wastelands.

For the green-backed heron (*Butorides striatus*), stealth is essential to hunting prey in the marsh.

PREFACE

An Invitation to See and Rejoice

Early morning on a winter's day and the sounds of the marsh surround me: the *scree* of the hawk, the *cheet-cheet-cheet* of the eagle, the breeze rustling the marsh grasses. Above my photography blind the sky resonates with the calls of migrating waterfowl: it is a visual and auditory experience that intrigues and endears.

My feeling on such mornings is one of tranquility, even though all about me a struggle is occurring. Here, as in most of nature's theaters, a timeless drama is unfolding. The wild creatures of the marsh begin another day in their continuing quest for survival, sustenance, and procreation. Ducks eat tender plants from the pond's bottom with their heads underwater and tails in the air. Wading birds search the shallows for fish, and hawks cruise over adjacent fields looking for rodents and other prey. The cycles of life continue here as they have since time began, and I am inspired.

My inspiration has driven me to photograph wetlands for many years. When I began in nature photography, my first subject was a swamp near my home. Its

dark and brooding presence called to me each day as I drove by and that fascination has never diminished.

The subject of wetlands is now so prevalent in the news that I imagine most Americans are aware there is some sort of problem. But what, exactly, is the problem, and why should Mr. and Ms. America be concerned about yet another environmental issue?

We live in a rapidly developing society and the momentum increases every day. In the future there will be more of everything, and there will be less: fewer forests and less clean air; fewer wetlands and less clean water; and less room for wildlife.

Admittedly this is a complex issue. Merely advising the public that another species of frog has been lost to extinction does not garner much concern. Most people do not become alarmed until it is apparent that such events indicate grim portents for the quality of human life.

In his text, Doug Phillips explains the subject of wetlands with an expertise and understanding far greater than my own. My wish is that my part of this project,

The parasitic dodder vine (*Cuscuta gronovii*) extracts its energy from the host plant. The dodder vine needs no chlorophyll. Instead of green, its color is orange.

the photographic images, will inspire readers to see more of the natural wonders portrayed.

Literature is filled with the words of poets and novelists who have found inspiration in these mysterious places. As a photographer—and lover—of all things natural, I too have long been fascinated by them. However, I find that many people think of wetlands as mosquito-infested places that should be avoided, not as places to be enjoyed. Photographers have long documented subjects that tear at the social fabric. In keeping with this tradition, I hope that my photography of the rare beauty I find in wetlands will change some readers' perceptions, encouraging them to seek out their own places of inspiration.

More than anything else, Doug Phillips and I hope that this book will instill in Alabamians, and readers everywhere, the sense that our remaining wetlands are a precious resource in need of nurturing and protection. May we always enjoy the lovely sounds of the marsh!

ROBERT P. FALLS SR.

Discovering

ALABAMA

WETLANDS

View of cypress swamp, Mobile–Tensaw Delta. Cypress trees, commonly viewed as symbolic of marshes and swamps, are among the oldest living trees in Alabama. These trees can reach more than eight hundred years of age.

INTRODUCTION

Wetlands — Where Lands and Waters Meet

ALABAMA RANKS AS ONE OF THE MOST naturally diverse states in the nation. A primary aspect of this diversity is Alabama's remarkable array of wetlands. The word *wetlands* refers essentially to just that—wet lands. For many people, the word brings to mind images of swamps and marshes. But the term encompasses a worldwide range of features with a variety of names, including bogs, mires, moors, sloughs, potholes, bottomlands, and bays. These wetland settings are typically shallow inundated or saturated zones where lands and waters meet.

The term *wetlands* does not apply to oceans, nor to the deep waters of large lakes and rivers or other reservoirs of significant size and depth. Ecological studies have established sophisticated criteria for identifying wetlands, and today the many different types of wetlands are described scientifically according to associated hydrology, soils, and vegetation.

This new understanding of wetlands is relatively recent. Historically the human tendency has been to see wetlands as wastelands, thus contributing to the widespread draining, filling, and polluting of these special habitats. More than half of our country's native wetlands have been lost to agriculture, industry, and commercial and residential development.

Fortunately, today's increased knowledge is bringing increased awareness. Now the word *wetlands* is often spoken with a new sense of urgency, as in "Save the wetlands!" This is especially true in places like California, where environmentalists lament the loss of riparian wetlands to agribusiness, and in places like the Dakotas, where duck hunters work to save prairie potholes, important wetland nesting habitat for much of America's waterfowl. Even in the grand metropolitan areas of such states as New York and New Jersey, concern is voiced for "urban wetlands," the scattered remnants of wetland settings that are the last vestiges of many important environmental values for city dwellers.

However, many of us in Alabama go about daily life with little thought to wetlands. The basic ingredient of

Adult common gallinule (*Gallinula chloropus*) teaches feeding techniques to newly hatched chicks.

wetlands, water, is quite abundant in the state. Thus the human tendency is to take these resources for granted. On the other hand, Alabamians have the advantage of noting environmental losses elsewhere in the nation and learning from the mistakes of the past. We have a timely opportunity to recognize the values of our wetlands and become proactive for their protection.

This opportunity also presents a challenge. Alabama today is increasingly attractive for new growth, including the same kinds of expanding development that have so extensively altered the native landscapes of other regions. Such growth will undoubtedly bring accelerating change to the Alabama landscape. Much of this change will pose potential risk to the state's wetlands.

The challenge of protecting our wetlands goes beyond saving a few unique features. Alabama's remaining wetlands will be essential to wildlife, water quality, economic stability, and the quality of life for generations to come. Sustaining these important values will require that we protect the ecological integrity of entire wetland systems.

The future of Alabama's wetlands is contingent upon public concern for this special resource. A first step toward ensuring such active appreciation is embracing the beauty and diversity of the state's wetland habitats. *Discovering Alabama Wetlands* is a labor of love intended to celebrate these aspects of Alabama's remarkable natural heritage.

Ducks in winter wetland created by seasonal lowland flooding, Jackson County.

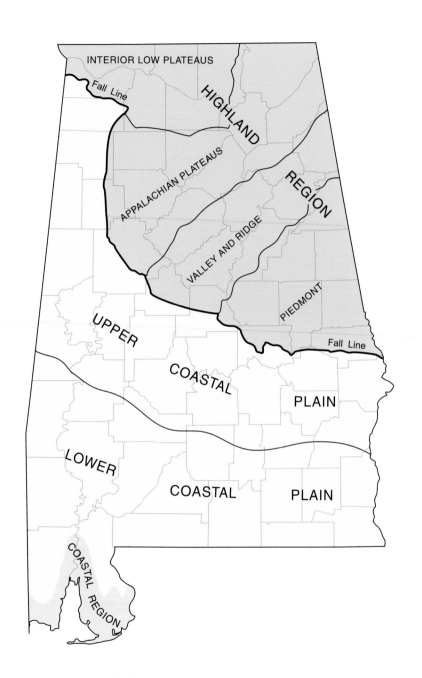

INTERIOR LOW PLATEAUS

Fall Line

HIGHLAND

APPALACHIAN PLATEAUS

REGION

VALLEY AND RIDGE

PIEDMONT

Fall Line

UPPER

COASTAL

PLAIN

LOWER

COASTAL   PLAIN

COASTAL REGION

Physiographic regions of Alabama.

CHAPTER ONE

ALABAMA'S DIVERSE WETLAND RESOURCES

Paradise is where I am. —Voltaire

ALABAMA'S VARIED WETLANDS INCLUDE most types identified by scientific classification. The scientific description of wetland types is discussed further in the next section. Meanwhile, Alabama's wetland diversity is also discernible in basic terms tied to the state's physiography. The physiographic regions of Alabama are shown in the map on the opposite page.

GEOGRAPHIC OVERVIEW: MAJOR WETLAND REGIONS OF THE STATE

A first physiographic distinction about wetlands is whether they occur as coastal wetlands or inland wetlands. Alabama's coastal wetlands are concentrated in Baldwin and Mobile counties, the only Alabama counties with coastline. Wetlands elsewhere in the state are more distant from the coast and are therefore considered inland wetlands.

Another major physiographic distinction about Alabama wetlands can be made between the two main inland portions of the state, which are separated by the Fall Line. The Fall Line is a topographic feature that traverses the entire midsection of the state and marks the boundary between ancient rocky strata of northern Alabama and younger, softer sediments to the south.

Thus, from north to south across the state, Alabama's wetlands are found in three general areas—the highland and Appalachian terrain of the upper part of the state, the rolling landscapes of the Coastal Plain, and the lowlands along the Gulf Coast. Wetlands in these three regions are affected by differing geological and hydrological conditions that typify each area.

Seasonal rains bring new growth of aquatic plants to spring-fed wetland, highland region.

Highland Region

The region north of the Fall Line is itself divided into four physiographic provinces: Interior Low Plateaus, Appalachian Plateaus, Valley and Ridge, and Piedmont. These four highland provinces share common traits of rugged, rocky terrain. In much of the region carbonate strata are also present, often fractured and cavernous. Wetlands in this part of the state are usually associated with the prevalence of upland river settings, including numerous reservoirs and impoundments, or with the scores of springs, caves, and other solution features in the region. In either case, this portion of Alabama pro-vides interesting and frequently contrasting settings for wetland habitats.

For example, wetlands formed around springs, caves, and sinkholes are often isolated and have an allure comparable to that of a mini-oasis in the midst of arid surroundings. There are hundreds of such wetlands across northern Alabama, occurring in conjunction with widespread karst geology that readily transmits groundwater to the surface.

Several springs, such as Cold Water Spring in Anniston and Big Spring in Huntsville, were instrumental in the settlement of surrounding communities and have lost much of their wetland character as these communi-

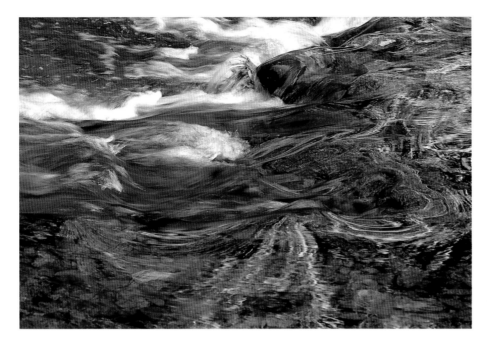

Water cascade in Autumn colors,
Little River, northeastern Alabama.

ties have grown. However, the majority of such features remain relatively wild and natural.

Many features are very remote, such as Annie's Springs, a beautiful seep at the base of a boulder-strewn hillside miles up an uninhabited valley in Jackson County. And there are many larger and better-known features such as Byrd Spring Swamp and Lake, a 600-acre Madison County wetland that receives its water from an adjoining cave.

In fact, Alabama caves often contain special watery habitats of their own, at times harboring endangered species such as the blind cave fish and the cave crayfish. Though not always classified as wetlands, such cave waters are evidence of subterranean hydrology that is vitally linked to the ecological health of surface wetlands.

The countless rivers and streams of northern Alabama trace their paths over striking terrain and, along the way, create wetland habitats specific to the region. A number of North Alabama rivers flow through upland forested valleys that qualify as wetlands because of periodic wet-weather flooding. Likewise, the lower reaches of many North Alabama rivers flood frequently, thus providing an additional kind of river habitat. Moreover, throughout northern Alabama the rocky topography of most streams is conducive to shoals and sloughs that often meet wetland criteria.

Green pitcher plants (*Sarracenia oreophila*). This wetland-dependent, endangered species is found in the vicinity of Little River Canyon in northeastern Alabama.

Among the more notable shoal features are the wide and lengthy shoals found at several places along the Cahaba River in Bibb County, and on Hatchet Creek east of Sylacauga. These are remnant examples of large shoal areas once common on many North Alabama rivers, and they also provide some of the last remaining habitat for the endangered Cahaba lily.

A host of interesting river-related wetlands in northern Alabama occur on public lands. For example, in northwestern Alabama are the wilds of the William B. Bankhead National Forest and its many watery realms, including the West Fork Sipsey River, at present Alabama's only National Wild and Scenic River. The Bankhead offers miles of pristine hardwood river bottoms, surrounded by a vast wilderness of fern-shrouded wet habitats.

In northeastern Alabama, Lookout Mountain is the setting for state and federal preserves adjoining Little River, which has carved the awesome Little River Canyon and is one of few rivers in the world to form and flow entirely atop a mountain. This dramatic feature is characterized by sculpted river niches of myriad shape and form.

Among the many river reaches of North Alabama, the Tennessee Valley is grandest in scale. Here humans and nature have conspired to create a series of impounded waters that provide an abundance of wetlands for waterfowl. The crown jewel of these wetlands is Wheeler National Wildlife Refuge, a 34,000-acre preserve established in 1938 as part of U.S. efforts to restore declining populations of waterfowl. The refuge, like other impounded areas along the river, comprises marshlands of seasonal depth and vegetation attractive to migrating species.

Other North Alabama river impoundments, like those along the Coosa and Tallapoosa Rivers, provide additional wildlife habitat and contribute to an estimated total wetlands area of more than 600,000 acres above the Fall Line.

The endangered Cahaba lily (*Hymeno-callis coronaria*) blooms along the shoals in the Cahaba River, in Bibb County south of Birmingham. This area of the river has recently been protected as a national wildlife refuge.

American coots (*Fulica americana*) on Guntersville Lake.

Tributary flowing into West Alabama's Sipsey River and surrounding swamp.
The swamp is recognized as one of the state's most significant wetlands.

Migrating snow geese (*Chen caerulescens*) take flight en masse, Wheeler National Wildlife Refuge.
Some will winter here; others will rest and continue southward.

Wetland-dependent cattails (*Typha latifolia*) in spring, Coosa River Basin.

Egret rookery and Canada geese, Gadsden Wildlife Park. Such roosts, surrounded by water, allow the birds to rest and procreate safely.

Autumn color in wetland of highland region.

Duck observation house, Wheeler National Wildlife Refuge.

There is a beautiful music that emanates from a flock of geese in flight, a haunting primal sound of nature like no other. This chorus of honking voices fills the winter skies over Wheeler National Wildlife Refuge in northwestern Alabama.

Waterfowl are the attraction here. The refuge is managed to support migratory birds from northern nesting grounds, as well as to protect endangered species. The visitor may view as many as 40,000 Canada geese and a small population of snow geese. There is also a cornucopia of ducks. The refuge's comprehensive bird list totals 304 different species, one of the largest populations along the North–South Flyway.

Like all other national wildlife refuges in Alabama, Wheeler is an excellent place to begin your wetlands experience. From the visitor center, you can take a short walk through lovely secluded woods to an observation building near a pond where waterfowl are fed regularly through the winter. The water's surface teems with activity, the sky is filled with arriving and departing birds, and all about the facility a miracle of nature is occurring. These creatures have traveled here from locations all over North America. Many have come from as far away as Canada's Hudson Bay region, navigating by means not yet fully understood by humans. When their offspring are hatched, the young birds will repeat the same journey according to patterns that predate human history by thousands of years.

Sandhill crane (*Grus canadensis*), a migrating species and occasional visitor at Wheeler National Wildlife Refuge.

Flood pool with duckweed (*Lemna sp.*),
Coosa River Basin.

Coastal Plain

Below the Fall Line lies Alabama's largest physiographic province, the East Gulf Coastal Plain. The name of this region is derived from its geological history of being awash with the last ancient seas to inundate the southeastern United States. The ebb and flow of these periodic shallow seas helped shape a more gentle landscape, upon which many rivers and streams have developed broad floodplains with important seasonal fluctuations in river levels.

Most wetlands in Alabama's Coastal Plain are associated with changing river levels in response to basinwide climatic conditions. Annual winter and springtime flooding immerse large areas, leaving water trapped by natural levees and perpetuating floodplain wetlands of several kinds, ranging from freshwater sloughs and marshes to bottomland forests.

Much of the nation's most abundant wetland habitat is found in association with Alabama's Coastal Plain rivers, along large rivers like the Tombigbee, Alabama, and Black Warrior, and along many smaller rivers such as the Sipsey, Conecuh, and Choctawhatchee. Here alluvial conditions nurture roughly 2 million acres of lowlands and river bottomlands, with cypress and tupelo gum often predominant in areas continuously wet,

Cypress tree (*Taxodium distichum*) and cypress knees on the lower Cahaba River.

and swamp oak, water hickory, sweet gum, and red maple prevalent on adjoining soils.

Coastal Plain hydrology also accommodates its own variety of isolated wetlands. These are typically associated with groundwater seepage, either at the bases of slopes or in depressions subject to groundwater inflow. Such seepage areas are often called bogs and support a surprising plant diversity, including many species of carnivorous plants. For example, several South Alabama bogs are nationally recognized for their populations of pitcher plants.

Coastal Plain wetlands are largely a function of the interrelationships between seasonal climate change, periodic river flooding, and subsequent water storage or "banking" in the broad watersheds of the Coastal Plain region. This hydrology is the basis for many contiguous wetland areas often linking bogs and shrub wetlands with grand forested wetlands. A key word here is contiguous. The Coastal Plain of Alabama contains some of the nation's last best examples of wild wetlands that are adjoining and continuous over large tracts. This is true for several Upper Coastal Plain wetlands, such as those of the 100-mile-long Sipsey River and Swamp, as well as for many Lower Coastal Plain wetlands, such as those of the vast Mobile–Tensaw Delta, which extends across several counties and into the present-day coastal region.

Pitcher plant bog, Conecuh National Forest.

Coastal Region

Alabama's coastal region is that part of the state bearing the most visible signs of ocean environments from recent geological time. That is, the coastal region can be understood as a large area (far more than the actual coastline) where geology, plants, and local variance in wind and weather are in close association with marine environs.

Of course, wetlands nearest the Gulf Coast are usually affected by ocean-driven tides. They are referred to as tidal and nonfresh (saline) wetlands.

As the crow flies from state line to state line, Alabama's Gulf Coast area is only about 70 miles across. However, the total distance of meandering coastline exceeds 300 miles and provides an abundance of some of the finest tidal wetlands in America. Here Alabama's beautiful beaches and dunes take the brunt of fluctuating tides for many bays, bayous, marshes, and mudflats still wild in setting and appeal.

Westward along the coast, barrier islands such as Dauphin Island and Petit Bois Island stand between deeper Gulf waters and scores of coastal habitats, from the salt marshes of Heron Bay to the pristine pine savannah of Grand Bay.

To the east, the white sands of Fort Morgan Peninsula, Gulf Shores, and Orange Beach provide wetland settings with remnants of once-majestic maritime forests. These meet the ocean ahead of numerous large, wild wetland systems such as Weeks Bay, Wolf Bay, Perdido Bay, and Lillian Swamp.

In the middle of Alabama's coastal area is the expansive estuary of Mobile Bay. The bay is fed by several small streams and associated wetlands around its perimeter, and is the funnel to the Gulf for seven major

Typical small coastal wetland,
Fort Morgan area.

river systems draining most of inland Alabama. These rivers merge at the upper end of Mobile Bay in a unique 200,000-acre geological depression called the Mobile–Tensaw Delta. This delta, second in size only to the Mississippi River Delta, is one of the most impressive wild wetlands in the nation.

Much of Alabama's coastal region is some distance from the actual coastline and less affected by tidal influences. Often these wetlands still qualify as coastal wetlands, though they are usually freshwater (non-saline) wetlands. For example, the Mobile–Tensaw

Delta extends north of Mobile Bay for roughly 50 miles. Its southerly juncture with Mobile Bay is characterized by tidal marshes with salt water and fresh water inter-mingling. Farther inland from the bay, however, the delta is predominantly freshwater forested wetlands, ranging from bottomland hardwoods to tupelo-bay and cypress swamps. Nevertheless, much of these freshwa-ter wetlands are considered coastal wetlands because of their close daily influence on estuary conditions in Mobile Bay.

It may be useful at this point to also mention a

Marsh and salt grass in summer, Mobile Bay area.

Coastal wetland, Bayou La Batre area.

statutory distinction regarding the state's coastal wetlands. Alabama's Coastal Zone Management Program defines the state's coastal zone as the terrain extending from saltwater shores (sea level, or zero elevation) inland to the 10-foot-elevation contour line.

In other words, for purposes of state regulatory authority, wetlands beyond the 10-foot contour line are not officially considered part of Alabama's coastal zone.

Of course, this demarcation is strictly for government use. It is not recognized by nature or, for that matter, by most wetland ecologists.

Taken together, Alabama's coastal wetlands—those above and below the 10-foot contour line—add up to an extensive area. If related resources such as oyster reefs are included, the total expanse of wetland-dependent habitats in coastal Alabama approaches 1 million acres.

The endangered brown pelican (*Pelecanus occidentalis*) is making a slow recovery in such areas as Alabama's Gulf Coast.

Golden club (*Orontium aquaticum*), wildflower typical of coastal wetlands.

High tide in the marsh, Dauphin Island.

Cypress swamp typical of coastal Alabama, Perdido Bay.

Green-backed heron (*Butorides striatus*) scans the wetland landscape, Bon Secour National Wildlife Refuge.

Alligator in camouflage, Eufaula National Wildlife Refuge.

Morning light on marsh grasses.

Wetland Types:
A Kaleidoscope of Nature

From her mountains to her beaches, Alabama's varied landscapes host an impressive array of wetland types. These are descriptive categories derived from scientific measures of wetland geomorphology, hydrology, chemistry, and biology. Put simply, in addition to noting differences of physiography and setting, specialists interpret wetlands according to specific parameters of soil, water, and vegetation.

Most wetland specialists distinguish one wetland type from another using systematic criteria such as those presented in *Classification of Wetlands and Deepwater Habitats of the United States* (Cowardin et al. 1979). These criteria were developed by the U.S. Fish and Wildlife Service to establish uniformity of concept and terminology in describing wetlands throughout the country. For the layperson interested in Alabama's wetlands, the major wetland categories of this classification system can be summarized as follows:

Marine: various ocean coastline environments
Estuarine: tidal waters of coastal rivers and bays, salty tidal marshes, and tidal flats
Riverine: flowing freshwater reaches of rivers and streams
Lacustrine: the shallow water reaches of lakes, reservoirs, and large ponds
Palustrine: freshwater marshes, swamps, wet meadows, bogs, pocosins, and small ponds

In the previous section, we looked at the diversity of Alabama wetlands in conjunction with the state's physiography. This physiography also serves as a backdrop for understanding and locating wetlands according to the categories of scientific classification.

The majority of the state's wetland acreage is palustrine, most often in the form of forested wetlands including cypress and gum swamps, hardwood river bottomlands, and pine savannah lowlands. Many isolated shrub swamps and seepage bogs also fit the category of palustrine wetlands. Palustrine wetlands are most abundant among the broad floodplains and watersheds of the Coastal Plain region.

Bald eagle (*Haliaeetus leucocephalus*) perched atop muskrat den.

Lacustrine wetlands represent another large proportion of Alabama's wetlands. These are distributed throughout the state in association with Alabama's major rivers, where many impoundments have created thousands of acres of lacustrine wetlands in the shallow areas of reservoirs.

Riverine wetlands also are widely distributed across the state, along flowing river reaches outside of reservoirs. Riverine wetlands are found in association with both the rocky, shoal character of northern Alabama streams and the slower, meandering character of many streams in the southern part of the state.

Estuarine wetlands occur exclusively in the coastal region. These are predominantly salt marshes of vary-ing characteristics along the state's many bays, bayous, and river deltas.

Likewise, of course, Alabama's marine wetlands are found solely at the Gulf Coast. These are saltwater tidal pools and basins of differing configurations that are exposed to waves and currents of the open ocean.

Thorough scientific description of wetlands is a complex process, involving a hierarchy of systems, subsystems, classes, subclasses, and various further divisions of even finer specificity. Such scientific detail has become increasingly necessary today. Precise delineation of wetland types and boundaries is often required to implement wetland regulations, guide environmental planning, and provide clarification in land-use decisions. Thus wetland identification is also frequently a factor in legal disputes when environmental interests and commercial interests collide over proposed development in wetland areas. In fact, wetland identification has itself become a major source of national controversy, as disputing parties disagree over the validity of how wetlands are identified and delineated. The attention given to wetland controversies in the media is a contributing reason for the growing public awareness of wetland issues today.

Those interested in learning more about the scientific classification of wetlands are encouraged to consult *Classification of Wetlands and Deepwater Habitats of the United States,* available from the U.S. Government Printing Office in Washington, D.C. For a look at the technical procedures of wetlands identification and delineation, consult the U.S. Army Corps of Engineers' 1987 *Wetland Delineation Manual,* available from the Department of the Army, U.S. Army Corps of Engineers, Washington, D.C. (also available on the Internet).

Meanwhile, with all due respect to the scientific community, the layperson is still allowed to speak of wetlands using plain old-fashioned labels. We can still call a wetland simply a swamp, a marsh, or whatever common name seems best to fit. Fortunately, an esteemed scientific agency, the Geological Survey of Alabama, has kept the layperson in mind while developing a modified wetland classification system for describing Alabama land cover. This recently implemented system is intended to facilitate computerized mapping of satellite imagery. Therefore, the system is simplified to provide a general level of description for five prominent wetland types in the state, as outlined below.

Freshwater marsh/swamp: Areas of fresh water that are mostly open, are relatively small, and contain floating vegetation and emergent grasses

Deciduous forested wetland: Typically river bottomlands with forest cover, primarily of deciduous (hardwood) tree species tolerant of wet soils

Mixed forested wetland: Forested lowlands that are very wet, may have standing water year-round, and are often dominated by needle-leaf trees such as bald cypress

Shrub/scrub wetland: Low areas with saturated or semisaturated substrate supporting tall grasses and woody vegetation that is typically less than 20 feet in height

Salt marsh/brackish marsh: Coastal area marshes containing salt-tolerant shrubs and grasses

Further information about this approach to classifying Alabama wetlands can be obtained from the Geological Survey of Alabama, P.O. Box 869999, Tuscaloosa AL 35486-9999.

Whether from the scientist's or the layperson's perspective, a kaleidoscope of natural variation and beauty awaits those interested in the state's wetlands. Alabama wetlands include just about every possible combination of scientific criteria and every imaginable array of wild wonder.

Common gallinule (*Gallinula chloropus*) feeding in marsh, Gulf State Park.

Duckweed (*Lemna sp.*) in quiet pool of Tennessee River backwater, highland region.

Ospreys (*Pandion haliaetus*) often nest in the tall trees in Mobile-Tensaw Delta wetland.

The Mobile–Tensaw Delta has many distributary rivers, streams, bayous, and creeks that form a maze of waterways. The delta begins south of the confluence of the Alabama and Tombigbee Rivers, which combine to become the Mobile River. The Mobile, in turn, divides into several major distributaries—the Tensaw, Appalachee, and Blakeley Rivers.

Located well inland from the sea, the Mobile–Tensaw Delta is not a typical river delta; it contains an unusual mix of wetland types. For example, one can view an array of riverine wetlands surrounded by countless swamps of palustrine wetlands. Where the delta's freshwater distributaries join saltier waters of Mobile Bay, a variety of estuarine wetlands can be seen.

The various wetlands in the delta provide habitats for an impressive diversity of wildlife, from ospreys to alligators. This expansive wild wonderland was a gateway to the American interior for many European explorers. Many of the native tribes they encountered had villages located in clearings along the rivers. One such tribe, the Alabamous, is believed to be the source of our state's name.

Spring scene, Little River Canyon Nature Preserve.

The endangered elf orpine (*Sedum smallii*), a wetland-indigenous plant, Little River Canyon.

Autumn leaves float on wetland pond, Oak Mountain State Park.

Dawn breaks over Mobile Bay bayou.

CHAPTER TWO

WETLAND VALUES

The nature of life is nature. —Liberty Hyde Bailey

ALABAMA'S VARIETY AND EXPANSE OF wetlands arguably contribute to every aspect of life in the state. With a cultural heritage linked to the land and an economic future tied to natural resources, Alabamians rely on the bounty of nature. The value of wetlands to this bounty might best be summed up in a word: sustaining.

ECOLOGICAL VALUES: WETLANDS SUSTAINING NATURE

The phrase "kidneys of the landscape" has been used so often to describe the role of wetlands that it has become somewhat cliché. Still, no single metaphor better dramatizes the importance of natural wetlands. As kidneys cleanse blood flowing through the human body, wetlands cleanse waters flowing across the landscape. Humans cannot live without kidneys; the native landscape cannot live without wetlands. Yet despite the potency of this metaphor and the importance of this cleansing capacity, they represent just one of the remarkable sustaining functions of wetlands.

Several factors coalesce across the landscape to produce the sustaining functions of wetlands. An examination of these factors reveals symbiotic relationships involving everything from the tiniest microorganism to the largest mammal. Only the sum of inseparable parts creates a system with the natural sustaining power of a wetland; for the sake of discussion, however, these factors may be considered individually.

Location

Between the terra firma and the rivers and lakes, there lies a zone of life that allows the terrestrial and the aquatic to merge harmoniously. On the terrestrial side of the zone live the plants and animals that cannot tolerate water-saturated soils. In the watery world of rivers and lakes are a host of flora and fauna that cannot tolerate many of the minerals, chemicals, and nutrients associated with the land. Strategically positioned, an inland wetland mitigates flooding that can be catastrophic to terrestrial life. At the same time, it prohibits upland contamination from reaching the aqueous realm.

Alabama's coastal wetlands are well positioned to face the fury of a storm from the sea. Coastal wetlands act more like sponges than like bulwarks against a storm. They absorb the storm surge, subverting its wrath and, in most cases, preventing it from wreaking havoc inland. Like their inland counterparts, coastal wetlands guard ocean waters from pollutants.

In scientific language, most wetlands are *ecotones* or transitional areas between adjacent habitats. This aspect of location usually means that an ecotone is especially rich in biological diversity. It also means that wetland ecosystems are positioned to provide many environmental services.

As the first layer of defense for a body of water, a

Immature Louisiana heron (*Egretta tricolor*) searches for prey in Gulf State Park.

wetland provides a repository for potentially harmful materials. Urban sprawl and agriculture generate a plethora of toxic by-products, which eventually penetrate the soil. With rainfall, these materials often wash directly into creeks, streams, and rivers as toxic mud.

Tidal pools in Dauphin Island marsh absorb storm surges, protecting the mainland.

Waters flowing off the surrounding lands may carry fertilizers and pesticides, treated and untreated sewage, industrial chemical waste, and increasing amounts of damaging sediments. These sediments can drastically change the ecology of a water body, altering flow and destroying indigenous life.

A wetland allows many of the contaminants from surrounding lands to settle before reaching a main body of water. Here these materials are assimilated and transformed to provide habitat for living creatures and become part of the complex wetland ecosystem.

Sands and Soils

Along with the sediment that is rain-washed from surrounding lands come many minerals, chemicals, and nutrients—both natural and artificial. A wetland's sands and soils act as a natural sieve trapping many of the larger pollutants. It's no coincidence that swimming pool filters and drinking water filtration plants use sand to perform this same purging process.

Soil type is a key indicator of wetlands. Wetland soils may be primarily mineral (including sandy varieties) or

Fragrant water lily (*Nymphaea odorata*), common to Alabama wetlands.

primarily organic. In either case, they must also qualify as *hydric* soils, which are saturated enough during the growing season to develop low-oxygen-producing (anaerobic) conditions that favor the growth of water-adapted plants. For example, the bottomland wetlands of the Sipsey River Swamp in West Alabama are supported by hydric soils of the Amy group. These are poorly drained soils in depression areas that are very suitable for water tupelo and other water-adapted trees.

There are seven major soil groups in Alabama, distributed in association with different geologic regions of the state, and each of these major groups contains many different varieties of hydric soils. A list of Alabama hydric soils is available from the U.S. Natural Resource Conservation Service.

Microorganisms

A myriad of microorganisms are constantly at work—the unseen heroes within a wetland system. Microbes, such as bacteria, protozoa, communal bacteria, fungi, and algae, thrive in a natural wetland environment. Nutrients and pollutants that might be devastating to a stream's ecology may be nourishment for a microbe. These organisms assimilate many nutrients and pollutants, detoxifying some and transforming others from inorganic to less damaging organic materials, and preventing them from traveling downstream. In addition, these microbes support an array of other higher organisms, invertebrates, and aquatic insects, all of which serve as food for yet higher animals.

Vegetation

A variety of vegetation assists in the natural sustaining role of a wetland. Vegetation provides sustenance and

Detail of dried wetland being filled in by sedimentation from agricultural and construction runoff.

Green-backed heron (*Butorides striatus*) feeding among water pennywort (*Hydrocotyle bonariensis*).

habitat for a melange of critters that make their own contributions to the system. The vegetation may feed on some of the nutrients and minerals that threaten a stream, whereas plants can act as anchors or dams, prohibiting sediments from reaching a stream; roots and fallen foliage can perform a filtering function.

The panoply of plant life is one of the more enticing features of an Alabama wetland. The state's coastal salt marshes are typically dominated by needle rush and giant cordgrass, with a host of lesser plants mixed in, including sea lavender, salt marsh aster, and spike grass. More than fifty herbaceous plants, grasses, sedges, and rushes are found inhabiting Alabama's saline and brackish marshes.

Among Alabama's inland freshwater marshes and deepwater swamps is an even greater array of plants. Freshwater marshes are adorned with such seasonal beauty as the blue flag in springtime and the mist flower in fall. Wintertime too can be intriguing, as freshwater marshes often contain rattlebox, arrowhead, and other interesting dressings of the season.

The vegetation of swamps varies to a large extent with the amount of water and frequency of flooding. Common tree types are many, including tupelo, bald cypress, water oak, swamp bay, and magnolia. Understory vegetation includes Virginia willow, yaupon, and fetter bush. More than 150 plant species thrive in Alabama's freshwater marshes and swamps.

Blooming water hyacinth (*Eichhornia crassipes*). This commonly seen plant is indigenous to Alabama wetlands.

Though common in occurrence, the water hyacinth is a wonder of rare beauty. Speaking of rare wonders, biological surveys reveal that around one-third of all threatened plants and roughly half of all threatened and endangered animals use wetlands at some point in their life cycles. Wetland-dependent flora and fauna are important ecological components in the web of life.

Many wetland inhabitants have genetic and chemical properties of potential benefit to humans. For example, a recently discovered protein in a salt marsh bacterium has been considered for application in the computer industry. The blood of horseshoe crabs is already used to test for various life-threatening human infections.

The role of wetlands in ridding our waters of pollutants is another ecological function. Many wetland plants, such as salt grass and water hyacinth, help to absorb excessive nutrients that would otherwise accumulate to toxic levels, harming both water quality and aquatic life.

A frog, high on the food chain, surveys its wetland environment from a lily pad.

Water parsnip (*Sium suave*) in North
Alabama wetland.

Virgin's bower (*Clematis virginiana*),
spring wildflowers in Gadsden.

Tidal floodplain and salt grass on Dauphin Island.

Mallard (*Anas platyrhynchos*), the most common duck in Alabama.

Wildlife

A flourishing wetland system is haven for a heterogeneity of animals, large and small. Many find a home; others visit periodically to forage and to drink of wetland-purified waters. These critters, too, contribute to the sustaining accomplishments of the system. Some contribute their own flesh to animals higher on the food chain. Some feed on and recycle the remains of dead plants and animals. Some dine on the vegetation, spreading seeds through elimination as they travel the wetland. Of course birds and bees do their part to propagate the system. Hundreds of animal species—indeed, the majority of animals in the state—use Alabama's wetlands, but of particular concern are scores of rare species.

Alabama wetlands are home to the last remaining populations of the Alabama black bear. This declining species, once an inhabitant of most of the state, today finds the rich wetlands of the Mobile–Tensaw Delta region to be its last safe haven against a crowding human society.

For similar and additional reasons, Alabama wetlands harbor a disproportionate number of threatened and endangered species of many kinds. At least a dozen endemic and threatened and endangered plant species are wetland inhabitants. Of the many dozens of endangered animal species found in Alabama, more than forty make their homes in wetlands. These include, for example, the Alabama red-bellied turtle, Bachman's warbler, and the slack water darter.

The preponderance of special animals dependent on wetland habitats suggests that Alabama wetlands are an ark of survival for much of the biodiversity in the state.

River otter (*Lutra canadensis*), a wetland-dependent animal found in most Alabama rivers.

Whitetail deer (*Odocoileus virginianus*), one of many animals dependent on wetlands for food and water.

Black bears (*Ursus americanus*) require large roaming areas.
Currently they find sufficient terrain for survival only in the Mobile–Tensaw Delta.

Sum of the Inseparable Parts

Together, a wetland's location, its role as a repository, its sands and soils, its microorganisms, its vegetation, and its wildlife total a system that sustains organisms within its boundaries and beyond. Perhaps the most obvious testimony to the far-reaching sustaining power of a wetland is water quality. Good-quality water in Alabama's creeks, rivers, and bays can be traced through healthy wetland systems. Wetlands help to lessen erosion, control flooding, and filter runoff from surrounding lands. The ecological upshot is the storage, purification, and replenishment of surface waters and the recharging of groundwater. Less obvious is the contribution wetlands make to clean air. Evidence is that wetlands play a role in restoring atmospheric balances that have been upset by human activities. Wetland components perform large-scale recycling of atmospheric contaminants. More than this, however, the role of wetlands in supporting the health of terrestrial and marine environments is crucial to global atmospheric balance.

From subsurface aquifers to stratospheric gases, wetlands are vital in sustaining our living planet.

Great egret (*Casmerodius albus*) takes flight, Gadsden Wildlife Park.

ECONOMIC VALUES: WETLANDS SUSTAINING SOCIETY

How much is clean water and clean air worth?

Attributing economic values to the role of wetlands leads to questions that will be debated long into the twenty-first century. Some consider the functions of nature's systems free services. Others see dollars in the form of harvested timber, agricultural growth, or real estate development. And then there are the arbitrary

Frozen pond surface, Oak Mountain State Park.

numbers government places on private land holdings in the form of property and inheritance taxes.

The very term *value* spawns debate. Does society have ethical or moral values that make it duty-bound to protect nature? Are inherent natural values in and of themselves worthy of attention? Do traditional American values such as private land ownership supersede all other considerations? Is monetary value the ultimate determining factor?

In an effort to preserve remaining wetlands and other natural systems, many conservationists and environmentalists have begun attempting to place monetary values on the functions of nature. Terms such as *natural capital* appropriate the terminology of economics. Bold statements have been made, for instance, "All the GNPs of all the nations on earth could not match the dollar value of the services provided by nature." This statement may well be true, and in the long run humankind may wish its significance had been better understood, but the statement falls short of addressing the here and now. The world is not losing its natural systems, wetlands in particular, all at once; it is losing them one wetland at a time. It is easier to understand and appreciate the relevance of a wetland's economic value when specific locales are examined.

When examining Alabama, one finds a direct correlation between a healthy economy and healthy wetlands.

Great egret (*Casmerodius albus*) in beaver pond, Coosa River area.

The egret, a superb fisherman, is one creature for which wetlands provide regular sustenance. Wetlands also support shrimp, crab, flounder, mullet, striped bass, and scores of other species, all contributing members of intricate food chains. However, wetland benefits to daily liveli-hoods are more often described in terms of commercial fish harvests. Directly or indirectly, wetlands provide about 75 percent of the nation's annual fish catch. Commercial fishing and sportfishing in the United States generate tens of billions of dollars per year.

Spring bloom on trees, Alabama River backwater.

Historical Perspective

Long before Interstate 65 or even U.S. Highway 31 existed, there were the travel ways provided by nature. Many prehistoric native peoples canoed the rivers; many more walked. The outer reaches of wetlands, spreading out along rivers and streams, made walking a lot more comfortable during dry seasons. Archaeology supports this contention. Further evidence is visible in the form of the mounds along the Black Warrior River at Moundville and at the confluence of the Coosa and Tallapoosa Rivers at the Fort Toulouse/Jackson State Park near Wetumpka. The prehistoric Indian mounds are relics of thriving cultures and centers of commerce. Their locations on the riverbanks indicate the importance of the rivers and surrounding wetlands to travel and trade.

When the first Europeans arrived with horses, they too preferred the paths of least resistance. Records show that Hernando de Soto followed established Indian trails along the rivers. As the young United States began to expand west, settlers were attracted to Alabama for its abundance of water. Certainly the rivers made it possible to transport agricultural products to the port at Mobile. More important, a bounty of potable water purified by Alabama wetlands made it possible to live.

The abundance of wildlife flourishing because of the state's wetlands attracted market hunters and commercial fishermen during the late 1800s. Mink, beaver, muskrat, raccoon, and alligator were pursued for their fur and hide. Whole populations of birds were decimated for decorative plumage. Bison, elk, bear, deer, and turkey were hunted to supply a growing nation's need for protein. Alabama's commercial fishing industry exported hundreds of thousands of pounds of fish annually.

Water flowing over stones, upper Cahaba River. Early settlement in Alabama
was prompted by abundant potable water and rivers for commerce.

Armed with the doctrine of Manifest Destiny, pioneers eventually settled across the North American continent. Needing wood for their new towns and railroads, they looked to the South and to Alabama. In the early twentieth century, harvesting of the bottomland hardwood forests of Alabama wetlands opened up this fertile land to farming. Agriculture and the timber industry became leading contributors to the Alabama economy as the state stepped to the threshold of modern times.

Today's Economy

Alabama wetlands still provide thousands of acres to timbering and farming as forestry and agriculture continue to be leading contributors to Alabama's economy. Dollar estimates of wetlands' value to these activities vary from source to source, but all sources agree that the value is immense. For example, the value of standing timber in southern forested wetlands is estimated to exceed $12 billion. Examined from another angle, the total economic impact of forestry and forest products industries in Alabama is greater than $10 billion annually, and they support more than 100,000 jobs. The contribution of wetlands to this economic impact is twofold: they provide a significant portion of harvested timber and a high-quality water supply for multiple forest-related purposes.

The supportive role of wetlands is similar in scale for many other major contributors to the state's economy. Industry, tourism, recreation—all are multibillion-dollar economic activities in Alabama. Wetlands support the needs of such key industries as electric power generation, paper production, commercial fishing, and food production and processing. By helping to ensure an adequate water supply, wetlands provide for by-products of industry and businesses throughout Alabama. Moreover, wetlands help control the waste by-products of these operations. For example, it is estimated that a 2,000-acre wetland performs pollution control services worth roughly $1 million annually.

Tourism has become, as the saying goes, big business in Alabama. Combined tourism activities represent one of the state's top economic contributions. As Alabama becomes increasingly known for its bountiful waters, tourists are drawn to these natural attractions. Today, even golf courses (*especially* golf courses) are a natural attraction for tourists. Like many other developed tourist settings, golf courses are often developed to incorporate the appeal of wetlands.

Outdoor recreation has long been a mainstay of the Alabama economy. Today record numbers of people, both from within and outside the state, are enjoying hunting, hiking, boating, fishing, bird-watching, camping, and swimming in the wildlands and wetlands of the state. Likewise, the combined economic impact from these activities is breaking record levels, again in billions of dollars annually. Wetlands' support of this economic value is encompassing and at times astonishing. For example, activities such as hunting and birdwatching are often oriented toward waterfowl. Alabama's wetlands provide prime habitat for Eastern Flyway populations of more than 400,000 geese and 3 million ducks.

Alabama's Economic Future

Agriculture, timber, industry, fishing, hunting, golf, recreation, and tourism are current activities for which price tags can be readily tallied. Alabama wetlands' role in sustaining these activities also can be easily understood. Calculating and understanding the future, economic or otherwise, is a different matter. An important part of this query hinges on the question, What role will wetlands play in sustaining Alabama's economic future?

Alabama is in competition with the world. Many places around the world extol an educated workforce. Others tout cheap labor. Some places vaunt transportation and communications infrastructure while others promote tax breaks. All boast of quality of life.

Often quality of life is measured in terms of cost of living, education, available housing, shopping malls, theaters, museums, universities . . . ; the list goes on and on. Quality of life encompasses all of the above, and much more. At its most basic, quality of life is breathable air and drinkable water. Wetlands' impact

Canada goose (*Branta canadensis*), Eufaula National Wildlife Refuge. Some members of this migratory species are year-round residents, popular with hunters and birdwatchers alike.

on breathable air is global. In other words, all of the wetlands across large areas, even across the globe, work together to restore atmospheric balances that are affected by natural events such as volcanic eruptions, and by human activities such as burning fossil fuels.

Typical cold, misty morning in a Gadsden Wildlife Park wetland.

Tiger swallowtail butterfly (*Pterourus glaucus*), a common wetland visitor in the South.

of healthy wetlands, this contribution to Alabama's quality of life is no less meaningful.

In cleansing the waters, wetlands contribute to quality of life at its most basic level. In providing a natural oasis, wetlands contribute to quality of life at its highest level. When asked what they like about living in Alabama, people who have come here from other states and countries often say, "In Alabama I can be away from the city and into nature within minutes." These are not the words of back-to-nature groupies, holdover hippies, or New Age spiritualists. These are the words of men and women who are testimony to a scientifically recognized need to be in nature. Even as the psalmists of the Old Testament relied on an understanding of nature to find the metaphors to communicate their beliefs, even as Christ spent forty days in the wilderness before beginning his ministry, so human beings have a need to find peace in natural surroundings.

How can we put a price tag on the presence of natural surroundings? It cannot be done. Still, it is a legitimate quality-of-life issue that a growing number of businesses consider as they analyze potential locations. It is also among the reasons that some businesses remain in Alabama.

Communing with nature takes many forms: a day at the beach, hiking the mountains, canoeing a river, hunting a trophy buck, photographing a rare bird, and, some would even say, playing golf. The opportunities Alabama provides for people to enjoy these activities—

This fact makes it difficult to gauge wetlands' contributions to clean air on local levels. Not so regarding water quality.

Decades of study provide scientific confirmation that clean water, or the lack thereof, can be directly and measurably attributed to conditions in surrounding watersheds and wetlands. Although it may be impossible to put a dollar figure on the water-cleansing power

The diminutive sora (*Porzana carolina*) breeds and nests in freshwater marshes.

without being elbow to elbow—are difficult to find in much of the rest of the world. As populations increase across the globe, this asset, enhanced by Alabama wetlands, will give the state a competitive edge in luring and retaining business.

True Value

Alabama's wetlands help sustain potable water, contribute to clean air, and support generous populations of wild flora and fauna. Alabama's natural resources, enhanced by its wetlands, have supported the area since prehistoric times. Alabama's wetlands embellish the state's quality of life. And like gold, diamonds, and other precious metals and stones, Alabama's wetlands are in finite supply. These anthropocentric points of view may lead to improved methods of placing dollar values on the resource, which may in turn lend credence to efforts to protect wetlands. Ultimately, however, the value of Alabama wetlands cannot be measured in dollars, for ultimately Alabamians' relationship with their wetlands is not economic; it is biological. The state's wetlands are an increasingly important, sustaining refuge for wildlife and human life.

Morning on beaver pond, southern Alabama.

CHAPTER THREE

TRENDS AND CHANGES AFFECTING WETLAND RESOURCES

Nature, to be commanded, must be obeyed. —Tennyson

WETLANDS HAVE BEEN AFFECTED BY MANY variables throughout time. Storms, climate change, sea-level fluctuation, and other natural processes continually contribute to increases or decreases in the number of wetlands from region to region around the world. So it would be inaccurate to suggest that human activities are the only cause of wetland losses. Then again, it would be ludicrous to minimize the fact that human society has caused extensive wetland losses in the past two hundred years.

Of course being human means having human limitations, among them imperfect knowledge. Another facet of the human condition is that we do not know most things until we have learned them. Apparently, as in the case of wetlands, some things take a while to learn.

The recognition of wetlands as a resource of high value is a relatively recent phenomenon, as are most laws and policies aimed at wetland preservation. Although wetlands are today a topic of national concern, this new interest comes after a long history of disregard.

The nation was established and settled without a thought given to wetland values. Indeed a major preoccupation of the time involved another value, freedom—including the freedom to exploit the country's vast and seemingly inexhaustible natural resources.

For a century or more, our young nation exploited its bounty of native lands and waters with unrestrained zeal. By the latter half of the nineteenth century, Alabama and many other states were suffering the multiple consequences of this unchecked exploitation—depleted

American coots (*Fulica americana*) in Wheeler National Wildlife Refuge. Like many other species, the American coot has benefited from efforts to restore wetlands.

forests, eroded soils, sediment-choked streams, and declining populations of wildlife, with numerous animal species already pushed to extinction. So rampant was the abuse of nature that this period of U.S. history became known as the Age of Extermination.

The situation was particularly ominous for wetlands. Not only did the nation exhibit little regard for wetland values, but the very term *wetland* was unknown to the American populace. In fact, the word did not emerge in the vernacular until rather late in the twentieth century.

Meanwhile, native wetlands incurred an extreme toll as they were drained, filled, and otherwise altered and degraded for the sake of "progress." The land comprising the lower forty-eight states originally contained roughly 220 million acres of wetlands. Since colonial times, almost 120 million acres of those original wetlands have disappeared, representing a loss of about 55 percent of the country's native wetlands. States with substantial wetland acreage, Alabama among them, have suffered the greater proportion of this loss.

Kingfisher (*Megaceryle alcyon*) searching for prey. The kingfisher's feeding grounds continue to shrink as wetlands disappear.

ALTERED STATUS: IMPACTS TO NATIVE ALABAMA WETLANDS

Wetland specialists estimate that before settlement, the land we call Alabama contained more than 7.5 million acres of wetlands. Today, with around 3.5 million acres of wetlands remaining, Alabama is par with the rest of the nation; that is, the state has lost more than 50 percent of its wetlands. In many ways, this loss gives testimony to the nation's history of treating wetlands as wastelands.

Historical Impacts

One of the first federal laws dealing with wetlands, the Swampland Act of 1850, described "swamp and overflowing lands . . . [as being] . . . wet and unfit" for productive value. This act enabled several southern states, including Alabama, to lay claim to vast wetland areas with the intent of draining and developing these lands.

Much of the development of wetlands during the 1800s was for agriculture. Because bottomlands are frequently the most fertile, many river-bottom wetlands and lowlands were converted to farmland.

Wetland losses from such conversions were soon compounded by another practice, the wholesale logging of Alabama forests. Once again, river bottoms were a prime target. Ancient hardwoods and cypress trees provided millions of board feet of timber to meet the needs of a nation now expanding quickly westward. Many forested wetlands were changed forever. Such extensive

Typical wetland in Coastal Plain region, polluted by agricultural runoff in Bibb County.

losses of native river-bottom habitats occurred that a remarkable bottomland resident, the ivory-billed woodpecker, was eventually pushed to extinction.

By the early 1900s, large portions of Alabama lay barren of all but the stumps of forestlands that once were among the most impressive in America. This practice of forest decimation was called "cut out and get out" because logging operations moved quickly from one forest tract to another, carelessly stripping the forests bare. Denuded watersheds washed millions of tons of soil and sediment into every adjoining body of water, smothering wetland habitats of many kinds.

Adding insult to wetland injury, another disruption to native wetlands occurred with the damming of many of Alabama's major rivers. First it was the Black Warrior River, initially impounded in the late 1800s by a series of federally funded dams. A few decades later, the Tennessee Valley Authority built large dams on the Tennessee River. By 1970 several agencies and organizations had joined in completing multiple impoundments on most of Alabama's rivers—the Coosa, Tallapoosa, Alabama, Tombigbee, and Chattahoochee.

The intent of these impoundments was to provide better control of seasonal water levels and to facilitate river commerce. The impoundments have served their purposes well and brought many benefits, from flood control to the generation of hydropower. However, the unhappy consequences for Alabama's native wetlands include the inundation and destruction of countless shoals, sloughs, and other native riverine habitats. With the disappearance of these habitats, so vanished a rich invertebrate fauna unmatched elsewhere in the world.

Of course historical impacts to native wetlands from river impoundment, agricultural development, and forest clear-cutting are a fait accompli. Further, these impacts can be viewed as part of the price of human progress, during times when the importance of wetlands was poorly understood. Perhaps many wetland losses could have been avoided had there been greater awareness. Perhaps not. We should also be mindful that, in some cases, the net result of lost native wetlands has included the creation of new wetlands. For example, the extensive wetlands of Wheeler National Wildlife Refuge were created by impounding the Tennessee River and are today valued nationally for their role in providing essential waterfowl habitat.

Morning mist on upper Cahaba River, one of the state's last free-flowing rivers.

The Modern Era

Today's salient concern is that the celebrated progress of our modern society poses continuing threats to remaining wetlands. For example, commercial farming and forestry have steadily become more and more mecha-nized. This has meant, shall we say, greater efficiency in converting wild lands to croplands and commercial tree farms. Studies indicate that continued conversion has been a primary cause of the destruction or functional loss of Alabama wetlands in recent decades. Part of the problem here is that these practices often occur in

Migrating blue-winged teal (*Anas discors*), Wheeler National Wildlife Refuge.

secluded areas. They are usually not in public view and have rarely been subject to media attention.

Another wetland threat has attracted much media attention and generated a high volume of public activism. During much of the twentieth century, a host of chemical pesticides, insecticides, and toxic wastes were haphazardly released into the environment. Thanks largely to Rachel Carson and her 1962 book, *Silent Spring*, the alarm was finally sounded, alerting the public that many of these chemicals are extremely deleterious to the environment.

DDT and a number of other compounds were banned from use. However, scores of modern chemicals also persist in the environment for long periods.

As they flow into streams and wetlands, they can accumulate to levels that are toxic to both wildlife and humans.

Alabama has been cited in national and regional assessments as ranking among states with the highest discharges of chemical toxins. In a study comparing southeastern states, the Legal Environmental Assistance Foundation reported that Alabama ranks highest in toxic releases to the environment (*Toxic Releases in Alabama*, August 2000). Fortunately, science is doing much to improve our understanding and control of the environmental effects of modern chemicals. However, other environmental effects of our modern age may be more difficult to control.

Winter in a freshwater marsh, central Alabama.

Healthy forestlands usually equate with healthy watersheds. However, watersheds that are denuded of protective vegetation are a major source of damaging soil and silt, which ultimately wash into streams and wetlands. Modern logging practices frequently incorporate voluntary best management guidelines that include leaving forested buffer zones along streams and wetlands.

Land cleared for commercial development, on the other hand, is an increasing source of sedimentation to these water bodies. Temporary controls such as fenced erosion screens and sediment catchment ponds often provide minimal protection if any. As growth and development occur in many parts of Alabama, state regulatory agencies with insufficient personnel and inadequate funding find this potential wetland threat difficult to monitor.

Autumn leaves on a pool that nourishes the surrounding wetland, Talladega National Forest.

Coastal wetland and live oaks threatened by commercial development, Baldwin County.

Future Projections

In many regions of the United States, the human population is increasing dramatically. Further, as all demographic studies show, our society is becoming more urbanized and suburbanized. Thus today the native landscape is often converted not to agriculture but to asphalt. Each year the United States paves enough surface to cover an area larger than the state of Rhode Island.

As the South continues to attract new growth, Alabama is keeping close step with this national trend. Despite the existence of rural counties with declining populations, in many ways Alabama is showing signs of joining rapid growth trends found in other regions. News stories regularly feature the problems of sprawl, traffic congestion, and environmental degradation in a number of Alabama counties. The U.S. Environmental Protection Agency has targeted several such areas in Alabama that are considered at highest risk for future wetland loss.

Bay Minette–Foley Growth Area, Baldwin County

Baldwin County is located on the eastern side of Mobile Bay; it borders the Gulf of Mexico on the south and Florida on the east. The county has a substantial amount of coastline, a large portion of Mobile Bay along its western border, and the Tensaw, Mobile, and Alabama

Alligator wallow, Mobile–Tensaw Delta swamp.

Rivers in its upper section. Baldwin County contains some of the most extensive and vital wetland acreage in the state.

In the 1990s the Bay Minette–Foley urban growth area was the second-fastest-growing metropolitan area in Alabama. It encompasses the towns of Bay Minette, Daphne, Fairhope, and Foley, all experiencing rapid growth due to their proximity to Mobile (all are within 35 miles). Gannett Fleming ranked the Bay Minette, Foley, and Daphne divisions as first, second, and third among forty-three Alabama cities with growth patterns that may adversely affect wetlands.

Residential, commercial, and industrial development account for the bulk of wetland loss and degradation in Baldwin County. Marina and golf course development in the Gulf Shores area poses significant threats to wetlands and water quality. Major oil and gas exploration has occurred in Mobile Bay and the Mobile–Tensaw River Delta, and additional dredge-and-fill operations for exploration and production are probable. Development along the eastern shore of Mobile Bay and around Perdido Bay is a serious concern, as is disposal into bottomland swamps of dredged material from coastal navigation channels.

Water hyacinth (*Eichhornia crassipes*) blooming in Choctaw National Wildlife Refuge. Downstream from the Tuscaloosa and Demopolis metro areas, the refuge is being polluted.

Mobile Growth Area, Mobile County

Mobile County is located on the western side of Mobile Bay. The Gulf of Mexico lies to the south and Mississippi to the west. The Mobile River and Mobile Bay on the county's eastern border contain extensive associated wetlands composed of bottomland hardwood swamp in the river delta areas, and salt marsh along the coastal margin. Wetland areas on the Gulf of Mexico include salt marsh and Gulf Coast savannah.

The Mobile urban growth area encompasses the cities of Mobile, Grand Bay, and Tanner Williams. Of the forty-three Alabama cities whose growth patterns may adversely affect wetlands, Gannett Fleming ranked Grand Bay and Tanner Williams as fourth and seventh, respectively.

Residential, commercial, and industrial growth are the biggest threats to wetlands in Mobile County. Oil and gas exploration and production in Mobile Bay and the Mobile–Tensaw River Delta are a continuing concern, as is the ongoing disposal of dredged material from navigation channels.

Tuscaloosa Growth Area, Tuscaloosa County

Tuscaloosa County is located in the west central part of the state, approximately 50 miles southwest of Birming-

American alligator (*Alligator mississippiensis*) in the Mobile–Tensaw Delta.
Once a threatened species, this wetland-dependent animal is making a strong recovery.

Wood duck (*Aix sponsa*). This brilliantly colored duck is the second most common waterfowl in Alabama. Its habitat is in constant jeopardy.

ham and largely in the Coastal Plain physiographic province of the state.

Bottomland hardwood forests constitute the primary type of wetland associated with the Black Warrior and Sipsey Rivers and their tributaries. Owing to the geology of the region, the floodplains adjacent to these systems are generally fairly narrow in the northern reaches of the county and up to several miles wide in the southern part. They provide flood protection and enhancement of water quality for downstream areas. Lake Tuscaloosa, located on the North River a short way from its juncture with the Black Warrior, supplies water for the city and surrounding communities.

The Tuscaloosa area is expected to undergo an escalating increase in population between the years 2000

and 2020. Impacts to area wetlands are anticipated to originate from a variety of sources, particularly from record rates of residential and commercial growth, including lakefront and riverfront development, and development along the Interstate 20/59 corridor. Moody Swamp, south of town, is currently under significant development pressure. Industrial growth and new road construction are major threats to wetlands along the Black Warrior River drainage area.

Prattville–Montgomery Growth Area, Autauga / Montgomery Counties

Autauga and Montgomery counties are located in Alabama's Coastal Plain near the confluence of the Coosa, Tallapoosa, and Alabama Rivers. Wetlands in the area are largely associated with the Alabama River and its tributaries. The relatively wide floodplains consist primarily of hardwood swamp forests and serve to enhance water quality. About half of the city of Montgomery depends on the Tallapoosa River for its water supply. The city uses the Alabama River for disposal of its wastewater.

The Prattville–Montgomery growth area is also expected to experience fast growth in the coming decades. Residential and commercial expansion is the main threat to area wetlands. Autauga Creek, which flows through Prattville southeast into the Alabama River, is expected to suffer impacts from this expansion. The growth of Montgomery is primarily to the east and northeast, which may cause additional impacts to the Tallapoosa River. Industrial development, particularly along the Alabama and Coosa Rivers, is also a potential threat to area wetlands. Sand and gravel mining operations and improper treatment of industrial wastewater are some industrial activities known to produce adverse effects.

Athens–Huntsville Growth Area, Madison / Limestone Counties

This area encompasses the western half of Madison County and the eastern half of Limestone County in extreme northern Alabama. Most area wetlands drain into the Tennessee River and its tributaries and are dominated by hardwood species such as tupelo, oak,

and sweet gum. There are significant tracts of tupelo gum swamp in the area. Several major creeks are spring fed and support highly productive wetland systems. In the northern sections of the counties, numerous lime sinks provide habitat for a variety of plants and animals.

The Athens–Huntsville area has long been a high-growth area. Here, prime farmland acreage has been increasingly converted to urban use over the past thirty years. As a result, residential and commercial growth are expected to cause the greatest impacts to area wetlands. Residential growth on the southern and western sides of Huntsville has already adversely affected some wetlands in and around the city, as has creek channelization inside the city limits. A major golf course expansion near the southern edge of the city is anticipated to create significant commercial development affecting adjacent wetlands. From time to time, proposals are submitted for the routing of new petroleum pipelines, roadway infrastructure, and other major developments that would threaten wetlands of Wheeler National Wildlife Refuge.

Decatur–Hartselle Growth Area, Morgan County

Morgan County in north central Alabama shares many similar natural features with Madison and Limestone counties to the north. Most of the area's wetlands are associated with the Tennessee River and its tributaries, although several isolated systems are also present.

With the Huntsville–Athens growth area located

Spring color in wetland area.

about 20 miles away, and Interstate 65 passing adjacent to Decatur and Hartselle, wetlands in Morgan County are expected to be affected by urban development.

Much development has occurred in the city of Decatur and this trend is expected to continue. Commercial and residential development, creek channelization, and road construction are the major impacts to wetlands in and around Decatur. Expansion of the same type is occurring at a slower rate in the city of Hartselle. The relatively flat topography and wide floodplains in the Decatur vicinity support important wetland acreage that is potentially threatened by urban development.

This is especially true for those areas associated with Flint Creek, Baker Creek, and Clark Spring Branch. Industrial expansion along the Tennessee River could also adversely affect adjacent wetlands.

Alabaster–Helena Division Growth Area, Shelby County
This area is located at the southwestern edge of the Appalachian Valley and Ridge physiographic province, where it meets the Coastal Plain. Most wetlands here are located along riverine corridors, in fairly narrow floodplains such as those of the Cahaba River and its tributaries. Here, the greater length of the Cahaba River represents one of the last undammed major rivers

Migrating lesser scaup (*Aythya affinis*), winter visitors to Eufaula National Wildlife Refuge.

in the state. It is an Alabama Exceptional Water and has been proposed for designation as a national Wild and Scenic River.

Meanwhile, the Alabaster–Helena area has been consistently ranked as the fastest-growing urban area in Alabama; much of this growth is due to the expansion of Birmingham, the largest city in the state. Interstate 65 is nearby, and development outward from the Interstate is expected to continue.

Related industrial and commercial expansion near the Cahaba River system poses additional threats: discharge into and physical disruption of the area's wetlands. Discharges from wastewater treatment plants and from various surface mining operations also adversely affect these riverine wetlands.

Dothan Division Growth Area, Houston County

Houston County is located in the extreme southeastern corner of Alabama in the Coastal Plain physiographic province. Wetlands are composed primarily of river bottomlands and cypress swamps are common. The riverine systems of Little Choctawhatchee River, Big Creek, and Omussee Creek support wetlands in and around the city of Dothan.

Residential and commercial development are the major threats to wetlands in the Dothan area. Most of this expansion is to the west and northwest, though some expansion is also occurring south of the city. The main wetland systems expected to be affected by this growth are those adjacent to Beaver Creek, Rock Creek, and the Little Choctawhatchee River.

The exquisite roseate spoonbill (*Ajaia ajaja*), occasional visitor to Eufaula National Wildlife Refuge. Water levels here are sometimes threatened by Atlanta's drain on the Chattahoochee River.

Natural wetland settings are often victims of urban sprawl. When watersheds get buried under layers of concrete, steel, and asphalt, their natural functions—water purification, and aquifer and stream recharge—become diminished.

The long-running water war between Georgia and Alabama are a case in point. The root cause of this dispute is the sprawling growth around Atlanta, now recognized by expert analysts as greatly exceeding the region's capacity to provide such environmental essentials as an adequate water supply. The feud between the states began in the early 1990s when Georgia officials announced plans to increase water withdrawals and possibly impound the headwaters of Alabama's Coosa and Tallapoosa Rivers. Alabama officials, fearing subsequent shortages of water supplies for Alabama communities, vehemently contested Georgia's plans. Negotiations over this issue continue at this writing.

Statewide Implications

As the foregoing examples indicate, much environmental stress will likely result from factors that are complex in terms of changing economics and demographics, and at a deeper level as well. Many elements of projected change in Alabama—population growth, expanding infrastructure, new industrial and commercial development, urbanization—are often considered desirable emblems of success in the tireless pursuit of New South status. For some people, the conscious desire for such change is an expression of their unconscious insecurity about self-image as a function of the state's image.

Of course each person is rightfully allowed his or her imagined insecurities. But the popular push for Alabama to catch up with more developed regions could contribute to the emergence of several new insecurities.

A pertinent concern here is with a foundational component of the biosphere, groundwater. In many Alabama communities, the majority of residents and businesses depend on groundwater to supply most basic needs. Wetlands provide a related service in catching and transferring surface water to recharge groundwater aquifers. In turn, normal aquifer levels serve to sustain subsurface conditions and to provide groundwater discharge beneficial to wetlands.

The implications are easily drawn. As wetlands are converted, groundwater aquifers suffer. As groundwater aquifers are diminished, wetlands suffer. As expanding human activities bring increasing impacts to both wetlands and groundwater, people will suffer. When the supply of clean water runs short, life is threatened. Now, this problem presents a very real insecurity.

Another actual threat to our security comes from higher zones of the biosphere. Atmospheric climate change is no longer hypothetical conjecture. Most scientists (and most scientific studies) support the need for deliberate actions to curtail such problems as acid rain and global warming. These problems are largely the consequence of an increasing human population with a proportionate demand for fuels, chemicals, and other products that result in the release of gaseous pollutants. In recent years, Alabama has indeed begun to catch up with more developed regions. Parts of Alabama now experience the same sprawl, traffic congestion, and ozone and air pollution that plague such New South centers of progress as Atlanta, Georgia.

In fairness to Atlanta, the community has been a regional leader—socially, culturally, and in many other respects. However, Atlanta's environmental leadership is far less impressive. A case in point is Georgia's unwelcome water demands on Alabama rivers, now the subject of angry strife between the states. This conflict is largely a consequence of sprawling growth around Atlanta, recently assailed by expert analysts as being one of the nation's most poorly planned, troublesome areas. Indeed, during periods of drought, parts of the Atlanta

Red-winged blackbird (*Agelaius phoeniceus*), commonly seen in wetlands year-round. Breeding pairs nest near bodies of water and raise two or three broods per year.

area sometimes have inadequate water for flushing toilets. Little imagination is required to grasp the essence of this predicament.

For Atlanta and other such high-growth regions, the preservation of wetlands is largely a moot issue. These areas often have no significant wildlands or wetlands left to preserve. Despite self-praise for being "world-class" communities, places like Atlanta serve to alert us of serious problems brewing. If nothing else positive, perhaps these environmental troubles hold the promise that we in Alabama will take notice and learn from Atlanta's mistakes. But are we learning these lessons? Apparently not.

For example, the EPA has flagged the Birmingham area as a prospective "nonattainment" site for the years ahead. This rating is assigned to areas that fail to attain standards for air quality. Again, the implications can be easily drawn. If we are adding new pollution to the biosphere while losing wetland systems that help remove pollution from the biosphere, we could end up caught in a squeeze for life.

The trends and changes affecting Alabama wetlands are numerous, but most derive from the fundamental human need to put food on the table and shelter overhead. The pursuit of these material necessities has boded ill for wetlands thus far and possibly will do so into the future. However, to draw connections between economic activities and environmental consequences is not to assign malicious intent to the human endeavor for material sustenance. Nor does discussing these realities mean denying other obvious connections, such as

Water snake (*Nerudia sipedon*) cruises pond in search of food.

how being kind to nature can cost money. Environmental protection is often dependent on having sufficient economic means to pay for protective measures.

No commentary on an environmental topic, wetlands or otherwise, would be fair without acknowledging the environmental improvements that have been achieved to date. For example, governmental and private interests have worked together to correct forest depletion and soil erosion caused in the twentieth century. In recent decades, particular progress has been made in controlling certain types of industrial pollution to air and water.

However, any prognosis for the future of wetlands must take into account a frank recognition of how modern society is changing native landscapes. This is important in planning for a healthy environment *and,* ultimately, for a healthy economy. Long-term economic sustainability depends on long-term ecological sustainability. Alabama's remaining wildlands and wetlands are critical to this interrelationship. And *that* is this book's major point of emphasis, leading us to the question of paramount concern: How can we retain our abundant wildlands in the face of present forms of accelerating change?

Crimson pitcher plant (*Sarracenia leucophylla*), Conecuh National Forest.

Autumn color on canyon
floor, Little River Canyon.

FOREVER WILD: PROMISE AND PROGRESS FOR WETLANDS PROTECTION

By definition, of course, native wetlands are those that remain essentially undeveloped. They are places where nature is generally wild and intact. Conversely, protecting native wetlands means keeping these places wild for the future.

The bad news is that Alabama has no state agency with direct, comprehensive control over the status and protection of the state's wetlands. In other words, there are no Alabama authorities for statewide wetlands regulation as there are, say, for highway maintenance, beautician licensing, or alcoholic beverage control. However, the good news is that many agencies and organizations are working for wetland conservation in Alabama. Part of this work is mandated by federal statutory provisions intended to curtail wetland losses. These provisions are contained in such laws as the 1972 Clean Water Act, the 1972 Coastal Zone Management Act, the 1986 Emergency Wetlands Resources Act, and the 1990 Food, Agriculture, Conservation and Trade Act.

Boat-tailed grackle (*Quiscalus major*) in Fort Morgan area. This species normally inhabits coastal marsh areas.

Statutory Overview

The most frequently used federal program is that described in Section 404 of the Clean Water Act. Under this section, the U.S. Environmental Protection Agency and the U.S. Army Corps of Engineers jointly oversee regulations for the discharge of dredged or fill material into wetlands, while several other federal and state agencies have authority for review and input to this program. The U.S. Army Corps of Engineers administers the permitting of proposed dredge-and-fill activities, a role some people find ironical given the Corps' history of damming and dredging U.S. waterways from coast to coast. According to present Corps leadership, however, that was then and this is now. Today wetland preservation is an official priority of the Corps.

Most agriculture and silviculture activities are exempt from Section 404 regulations. However, provisions in the Food, Agriculture, Conservation and Trade Act discourage alteration of wetlands for agricultural use. Several of these provisions are administered by the U.S. Natural Resources Conservation Service and include subsidy incentives for preserving wetlands. Also, farming and forestry activities are subject to voluntary guidelines that are strongly encouraged by governmental agencies and industry groups. For example, the Alabama Forestry Commission promotes best management practices and streamside management zones (BMPs and SMZs, respectively) to help control stream and wetland impacts from logging operations.

The Alabama agency charged with primary powers of environmental regulation is the Alabama Department of Environmental Management (ADEM). Much of ADEM's role in wetlands protection is indirect, through its authority for implementing water-quality regulations required by the Clean Water Act. A related Alabama law, the Alabama Water Pollution Control Act, defines ADEM's statewide jurisdiction for controlling pollutants in all state waters, but the act carries no provision defining or protecting wetlands for their inherent value. On the other hand, the Alabama Coastal Zone Management Act underscores certain ADEM powers for identifying and regulating coastal wetlands. These reinforce federal regulations pertaining to dredging, filling, diking, excavating, and other permitted activities.

Meanwhile, the Alabama Department of Economic and Community Affairs is charged with planning for the use and protection of the state's water resources. The department periodically highlights wetland issues in its Statewide Comprehensive Outdoor Recreation Plan, as required by the Emergency Wetlands Resources Act. In recent years, the department's Office of Water Resources has devoted most of its time to the Georgia–Alabama water wars, a long-running dispute over water rights for streams such as the Tallapoosa River, which are shared by both states. However, this office is presently crafting a statewide initiative for long-term water management in Alabama.

The intent of present laws and regulations is to minimize destructive impacts to wetlands. A corollary to wetlands regulation is a strategy called wetlands mitigation. Recent federal policies require that new development projects comply with a three-step process for mitigating wetland impacts. First, potential adverse impacts must be avoided to the maximum extent "practicable." Second, any remaining unavoidable impacts must be minimized to the extent "appropriate and practicable." And finally, when unavoidable impacts occur, "compensatory" mitigation is required.

At first blush, such an approach seems quite logical. However, the concept of wetlands mitigation has been subject to differing interpretations regarding terminology, and, more important, regarding effectiveness in curtailing wetland impacts. For example, one means of providing compensation for wetland loss at a development site is to allow developers to restore degraded wetlands, or even to create wetlands at another site. An additional option is wetlands banking, whereby wetlands can be restored, created, or preserved, and their habitat values assigned to an inventory, that is, a bank, for possible compensatory mitigation in advance of future losses.

These strategies offer potential advantages, including possible consolidation of new wetlands into contiguous parcels, benefiting resource managers; and possible reduction of the time necessary for project approval, benefiting developers. However, an obvious downside is that current methods of mitigation equate with the ongoing, officially permitted loss of existing natural

Snowy egret (*Egretta thula*) in Bon Secour National Wildlife Refuge. The facility works closely with local organizations to protect wetlands.

wetlands. A related concern is that particular species and habitat conditions lost at development sites might not occur at corresponding mitigation sites.

Wetlands experts point to the absence of clear, scientifically acceptable methods to evaluate these factors. Further, available studies report substantial inadequacies, and, in some cases, the outright failure of mitigation efforts. As one scientist put it, wetlands mitigation has been an unmitigated disaster. Not everyone holds such a harsh view. Nevertheless, the question remains open as to whether wetlands mitigation can truly compensate for the continuous losses resulting from permitted impacts to our remaining native wetlands.

Voluntary Initiatives

The promise of government environmental policies and programs is that wetland losses will be reduced. Thanks to the dedicated efforts of many officials, this promise is not being forgotten. Yet in some respects, the greatest progress in wetland protection has come from private initiatives, spearheaded by organizations active on behalf of Alabama's natural environment. Among these groups are the Alabama Environmental Council, the Sierra Club, the Alabama Wildlife Federation, the Cahaba River Society, the Alabama Rivers Alliance, the Coastal Land Trust, and The Nature Conservancy.

Each group has a different set of environmental projects and priorities, but all share the priority of wetland protection.

In 1992, after a decade of completing preliminary groundwork, leaders from these groups joined representatives of business, industry, and state government in establishing Alabama's Forever Wild program. This unique land-acquisition program has forged broad consensus for state purchase and protection of special wildlands in Alabama. Already the program has acquired a number of critical wetlands. These include several thousand acres of the Sipsey River Swamp in West Alabama and a major purchase of 36,000 acres of the remarkable Mobile–Tensaw Delta in South Alabama.

The nationally recognized Forever Wild program, administered by the Alabama Department of Conservation and Natural Resources (ADCNR), operates under authority of an appointed board of directors. ADCNR has responsibility for managing state parks, wildlife, fisheries, and additional state-owned lands of various kinds. Forever Wild's board of directors, composed of scientists, citizens, and conservationists representing diverse organizations, meets quarterly to select priority wildlands for state purchase. The job of evaluating and surveying these selected lands is performed by specially trained personnel within the State Lands Division of ADCNR. The division's Natural Heritage Section maintains a statewide database of important habitats and natural areas. Working together, private groups, agency

The wetland-dependent northern harrier (*Circus cyaneus*) could become extinct along with the habitat that supports it.

officials, and specially trained biologists and data managers are achieving protection for Alabama's wetlands in the ideal way—by keeping these lands forever wild.

Wetlands being preserved by the state can now be counted with those managed by federal agencies on a range of public lands in Alabama. The U.S. Forest Service oversees wetlands in five national forests containing

Pastel colors of spring in an Etowah County wetland.

more than 600,000 acres and more than a thousand miles of rivers and streams. The U.S. Fish and Wildlife Service manages 55,000 acres on five national wildlife refuges in the state, of which roughly 50 percent are wetlands. The Tennessee Valley Authority maintains several thousand acres of wetlands in northern Alabama. In addition, the U.S. Army Corps of Engineers manages fourteen river impoundments in the state and more than one hundred public-use areas, many containing wetlands.

Public Education and Involvement

Beyond the existing regulations and protection programs are other signs of promise and progress for wetlands in Alabama. Not the least of these is greater public appreciation of wetlands. The credit for much of this new awareness goes to several home-grown groups working wholly for the cause of environmental education.

In recent years Alabamians have benefited from educational outreach provided by such organizations as the

Environmental Education Association of Alabama (EEAA), Legacy, Partners in Environmental Education, and the Alabama Collaborative for Environmental Education. Likewise, Alabama's schools and communities have learned about the state's remarkable natural history from such environmental education resources as the Alabama Public Television series, *Discovering Alabama*.

A most exciting example of public awareness is the successful Alabama Water Watch. This program, germinated from a small state grant, has grown into a large network of citizen volunteers who regularly monitor water quality throughout Alabama. The volunteers are trained and given necessary monitoring equipment. In return, they supply Water Watch and its parent agency ADEM with valuable data to help protect rivers, lakes, and wetlands.

Alabama is also home to a host of environmental centers, museums, zoos, parks, and university-based programs that promote wetlands research and education. Several of these are of national distinction. The Alabama Museum of Natural History at the University of Alabama is one of the nation's oldest museums of natural history. Since its creation in 1873, the museum has been a leading repository for research and education about Alabama's natural diversity. The university's Department of Biological Sciences now boasts an aquatics research program of world acclaim. A prime component of this program is the study of wetlands ecology.

Wetland-dependent star rush (*Rhynchospora latifolia*), Conecuh National Forest. This spring-blooming plant survives only where the water table is regularly above ground level.

Across the state, the Auburn University Fisheries Program has long been recognized for its investigation of many wetland-related needs for healthy fish populations. Auburn University's combined Environmental Institute and Water Resources Research Institute provide another valuable service, conducting the annual Alabama Water Resources Conference. The conference brings together state and federal officials, regulatory specialists, scientists, and concerned citizens who share vital information for managing water resources.

American alligator (*Alligator mississippiensis*), Mobile–Tensaw Delta.

Down at the southernmost tip of the state is the Dauphin Island Sea Lab, operated in collaboration with a consortium of Alabama universities. The lab is a model facility in a special setting: Dauphin Island is a national treasure of coastal history and heritage. Scientists, teachers, and students from throughout Alabama and the nation come to the Dauphin Island Sea Lab to participate in a variety of programs involving wetlands research and education.

Just a hop across Mobile Bay from Dauphin Island is another model program in another wonderful wetland setting. Weeks Bay National Estuarine Research Reserve was initiated by local folks, including leaders of The Nature Conservancy and faculty members from

nearby Faulkner State Community College. Because of their love for Weeks Bay, this area is now a nationally protected wetland with a well-equipped visitor education center used regularly by schools and other groups.

Weeks Bay National Estuarine Research Reserve is part of a nationwide program of protected estuaries administered by the National Oceanic and Atmospheric Administration (NOAA). This program reflects the growing attention being given to coastal and marine environments. In Alabama, additional U.S. research involvement is seen, for example, in the EPA-sponsored Coastal 2000 program and in several other coastal-area projects receiving federal support.

A complete listing of wetland-related laws and

Wetland in spring, Gulf Shores area.

programs is beyond the scope of this book. However, it seems appropriate to conclude by mentioning one of the best. Since its creation in 1848, the Geological Survey of Alabama (GSA) has been involved in the study of Alabama's natural resources. GSA's research provides information to assess needs and solve problems affecting Alabama water resources. The agency regularly monitors groundwater and surface water quality and maintains the state's most comprehensive water-use database. As funding is available, GSA also provides expertise for the inventory and mapping of Alabama wetlands.

Alabama is uncommonly blessed with an abundance of water, streams, and wetlands. It is only fitting that the state be abuzz with people taking note of these resources. Thus on any given day there may be a team of herpetologists surveying marine turtles at Bon Secour National Wildlife Refuge on Fort Morgan Peninsula, or

a class of high-school students studying the bluff-draped beauty of Hurricane Creek in Tuscaloosa County. There may be ichthyologists sampling fish populations along the pools and freshets of the Locust Fork River in Blount County, or concerned volunteers sampling water quality in Lake Martin. There may be university ecologists conducting a research project in the marshlands adjoining Payne Lake in Hale County, or a group of elementary-school teachers on a field trip in search of rare frogs in a Conecuh County bog.

Many of the gains in wetlands protection stem from the growing realization that the quality of our lives is linked with the amazing realm of wetlands. If we are to maintain a high quality of life in Alabama, we must continue the quest to protect Alabama's native wetlands. Today we can be proud of our progress, but tomorrow brings new challenges.

Cypress swamp in
Mobile–Tensaw Delta.

Alabama's Forever Wild program is nationally recognized as a successful model for state land protection. A state referendum establishing the Forever Wild program passed with a 90 percent voter approval, the largest favorable vote ever recorded in the United States for a state-sponsored environmental program. The program's purchase of almost 36,000 acres of the Mobile–Tensaw Delta represents one of the largest state land acquisitions in Alabama history. To date the program has acquired seventeen separate tracts, representing significant wildlands in every part of the state, for a statewide total of more than 50,000 acres now protected as forever wild.

Coastal wetland near Weeks Bay National Estuarine Research Reserve, Bon Secour.

CONCLUSION

A Heritage in the Balance

Now we face the question whether a still higher standard of living is worth its cost in things natural, wild, and free. —Aldo Leopold

THERE IS A DANGER IN EXTOLLING THE wonders of Alabama: if large numbers of people learn about the state's natural appeal, over time this could attract multitudes of new residents to Alabama. Continuous population growth can be environmentally destructive, particularly in a state with no comprehensive planning and few powers for controlling land use or guiding growth. On the other hand, there is great risk in not celebrating Alabama's natural qualities. Failing to arouse public concern for protection of these qualities might also result in the eventual loss of important wildlands.

This is a peculiar conundrum. Should we advertise the native wonders of our state or remain carefully mum—how can we know which is environmentally better for the long term? If we hail the natural glories of the state, should we also point to threats of degradation and impending loss—how can we give witness to both realities without seeming contradictory?

This dilemma has dogged producers of the state's award-winning environmental television series, *Discovering Alabama,* since its inception in 1985. However, the experience of producing *Discovering Alabama* on location in every part of the state confirms an overriding truth. Most Alabamians want the state to retain its abundant natural surroundings, and many also feel a sense of urgency about the need for wider awareness and stronger policies to prevent the loss of these surroundings. Increasingly, a priority concern is for preventing the loss of Alabama's wetlands, even if this means highlighting the wonders of these wetlands while simultaneously warning of their potential demise.

93

A New Scenario

The experience of producing *Discovering Alabama* confirms another Alabama truth as well. Every audience is eager to learn about the state's impressive natural qualities, but some audiences are less comfortable confronting certain questions about the future of these values. For example, Alabama's natural wonders are frequently touted by officials who seek new growth and development for the state. But how can we control growth to maintain abundant wildlands? This is often a secondary consideration at best.

Likewise, the natural features of Alabama are actively promoted as a draw for tourism. Tourism, of course, can be an environmentally friendly form of economic activity, but a question applies here, too. While we are spending millions of dollars promoting the use of Alabama's environment, how might we similarly promote environmental protection, including protection against growth and population pressures that will predictably follow successful tourism promotion?

These questions might seem premature, given that Alabama is still largely rural and in need of economic improvement. However, such concerns are quite timely for one main reason—Alabama's special qualities are being recognized around the nation and the world during a period when the South is experiencing rapid growth, populations are expanding dramatically, and change is accelerating.

There was a period not long ago when many people were leaving Alabama, claiming the state was "behind." Today Alabama's rate of population growth is surpassing the national average for the first time in modern record. This growth is punctuated by the arrival of new business and industry, including such prominent international stars as Mercedes–Benz. In part, this new attention is in response to the state's rural qualities and the abundance of forests, streams, wetlands, and wildlife. Some of the very features once thought to mar the image of Alabama are now seen as especially appealing. People are discovering that having plenty of backwoods does not make Alabama backwards. Being largely rural does not mean being behind.

To the contrary, today these qualities help put Alabama ahead of regions that have experienced more extreme environmental losses. One might be tempted even to question the need for aggressively (and expensively) promoting Alabama around the world. With all of its appeal, the state is going to attract growth whether we actively seek it or not. In this context, present progress in protecting Alabama's wildlands and wetlands may prove to be woefully insufficient.

Political Realities

In 1990 President George Bush acknowledged the urgency of wetland losses in the nation and expressed his support for a new national wetlands policy: "My

Snapping turtle (*Chelydra serpentina*) in Gadsden-area wetland.

position on wetlands is straightforward: all existing wetlands, no matter how small, should be protected." Such a policy would indeed seem straightforward and worthy of broad support. However, in the years since Bush's pronouncement, all manner of difficulty and debate have ensued. Confusion has arisen over which lands meet legitimate criteria for wetlands status. Disagreement has developed over jurisdictional responsibilities for managing wetlands. Angry conflict has flared over issues of private property rights versus governmental actions for environmental protection.

In Alabama the matter of government intrusion on private property is especially contentious. Alabama activists for private property rights have helped organize nationwide movements to counter federal provisions for recovering endangered species, saving rivers, and protecting wetlands. Central to the property rights movement are fears that Uncle Sam wields excessive power to usurp property values from landowners.

For example, if an environmental law prohibits cutting the nesting trees of an endangered woodpecker, this is seen as an unjust government "taking" of commercial timber value from the landowner. Likewise, should a farmer be prohibited from plowing a wetland

Marsh rabbit (*Sylvilagus palustris*) hides from alligators in marsh grasses.

meadow, this would be tantamount to robbing the farmer of the constitutional right to develop private property.

These fears are not entirely unfounded. In some cases private property owners have endured hardship and expense in complying with environmental laws to protect natural habitats. These instances are rare, however, and usually involve odd circumstances or misunderstandings that compound the situation. Nevertheless, property rights groups have stoked a deeply held angst among many Alabama landowners, resulting in a rather strong political force standing guard against perceived environmental excesses.

Now, this does not mean that property rights advocates are necessarily insensitive or uncaring about the environment. Alabama landowners typically feel a close

bond with the state's woods, waters, and wildlife, often a much closer bond than is felt by the modern urbanite. In fact, private landowners can be credited with the healthy status of many of the native wildlands that exist in Alabama today. Many Alabama farm and forest landowners faithfully follow environmental guidelines such as those in the state's voluntary program of best management practices.

As we look to the future, this set of circumstances is at once encouraging and disconcerting. Private land ownership accounts for more than 95 percent of the Alabama landscape and includes the majority of Alabama wetlands. Caring landowners who practice voluntary environmental stewardship represent the best of the American spirit. However, under present norms of the free-market system, natural values that are difficult

Great blue heron (*Ardea herodias*) searches for food in Demopolis wetland.

to quantify monetarily often lose in the tradeoff for short-term commercial gain. This has been the subtext of most of the nation's wetland losses through history. Caring landowners notwithstanding, why should we expect this reality to change anytime soon?

Put another way, the future of Alabama's wetlands is tied predominantly to the future of Alabama's private lands. This is the arena in which the challenges loom largest. Documented past trends and changes to wetlands are disturbing. Anticipated trends and changes could be devastating. The flavor of this potential change is evident, for example, at the typical economic development pep rally. Most such meetings and conferences in Alabama are led by chants for new highway construction, regional shopping malls, international airport development, industrial corridor promotion, and, for

many communities, some riverfront "improvement" thrown in for good measure. Sometimes a murmur about "protecting the environment" or "maintaining a sense of place" might also be heard. Just how such afterthoughts can be honored amidst radical rearrangement of both environment and place is a dilemma left for environmental groups to resolve.

A Frank Assessment

The future of Alabama's wetlands is contingent upon how we determine the highest and best uses of Alabama's private lands. Even the most environmentally concerned private landowner must survive economically. If the landowner's greatest incentive is to sell or otherwise convert native wildlands for commercial development, you can safely bet your investment portfolio on the likely fate of such lands. What are we in Alabama doing to counterbalance prevailing mindsets that zealously pursue expansive growth and development without giving equal commitment to environmental concerns? This is where the challenge of protecting wetlands becomes especially difficult.

In 1995 a team of resource specialists, including Alabama's best and brightest wetlands experts, completed a thorough examination of the state's capabilities to meet this challenge. In its findings the team asserted that, as Alabama enters the new millennium, its remaining wetlands are at increasing risk. The team's report cited the following problems:

- Alabama has no comprehensive state wetlands policy. There is no statewide wetlands conservation plan. Alabama laws and regulations do not explicitly and consistently address wetlands issues.

- State wetlands regulatory provisions are uncoordinated and fragmented. There is no statewide program to assess and monitor wetlands. Regulations do not consider the role of wetlands in supporting ecosystems.

- The number of state regulatory personnel trained in wetlands issues is insufficient to effectively protect wetlands. There are few nonregulatory methods and programs available to assist wetlands protection on private lands. The state of Alabama owns or manages a relatively small proportion of the state's wetlands.

- Few educational materials about Alabama wetlands are widely available. No effective environmental education program has been officially adopted by the Alabama Department of Education for use by K–12 students, nor has any training program for environmental education been adopted by Alabama's teacher training colleges.

- Most of the Alabama legislature, most state agency heads, and most local officials have no education or training in the environmental field, nor do they have ready access to an independent source of sound information on wetlands issues.

So here we are, in a state with uncommon natural wonders, where most Alabamians desire the protection of Alabama's rural and outdoor qualities. Much of the world is beginning to look upon us in envy because of our abundant natural surroundings. Here we are, in a state that is blessed with water and that contains much of the best of America's native wetlands. Here we are, with such a precious heritage at stake and yet unprepared to fully protect it.

This situation is compounded by myriad factors; no purpose is served by pointing a finger of blame. Rather, we should look to how the situation might be corrected. Alabama must find ways of ensuring a healthy economy

Cypress swamp, Mobile–Tensaw Delta.

Laughing gulls (*Larus atricilla*) bathing at Gulf State Park.

Great egret (*Casmerodius albus*) soars over Gadsden-area wetland.

that are in harmony with the natural environment and its preservation. Achieving such a balance will require much more than anti-litter campaigns and recycling programs. The foremost need is for political leadership with broad vision. Of course, political "leaders" are usually artful *followers*. They follow the direction of greatest public pressure. Therefore, the citizens of Alabama can do the most to protect Alabama's wetlands by firmly expressing their environmental concerns to state and community leaders. This can be done in strategic ways—by organizing, using the media, and simply letting friends, neighbors, ministers, and others know of pertinent concerns for Alabama's natural heritage.

Challenge Equals Opportunity

Science is telling us that protecting wetlands requires protecting entire wetland systems. Environmental and biological functions of wetlands are best maintained by ensuring the natural integrity of the supportive ecosystems, by saving intact, extended portions of watersheds.

History tells us that our native surroundings provide identity and a sense of place for who we are as a people. In other words, our natural heritage has helped to shape our cultural heritage. Alabama's abundant natural surroundings have played an important role in nurturing community values, enabling a pleasant pace of life, and maintaining important traditions and freedoms. These freedoms include access to clean air, clean water, and ample open space, as well as to wild wonders representative of America the beautiful.

Clearly what is at stake is much more than a scattering of unique sites. In protecting our wetlands, we are protecting more than attractive wildlands and nature preserves. We are protecting a heritage that is fundamental to a way of life and to life itself. As expanding growth and change come to Alabama, this special heritage hangs in the balance.

What will the landscape of Alabama be like twenty, fifty, or one hundred years from today? Will we be able to maintain our rural countryside and keep our wildlands intact? Or will Alabama become like so many other places, developed and artificialized to the point of losing close connection with its native natural heritage?

How successful will we be as stewards of our lands and waters? Already we must travel farther and farther to catch the scent of the marsh mallow, to witness the tricks of the mud snake, or to listen to the arguments of the frogs around a marsh at night. Indeed, for much of today's urban society such experiences are but memories from childhood, from times past and countrysides vanished. Yet we in Alabama are blessed to have so much remaining of our remarkable natural heritage. Thus we have the opportunity not only to experience Alabama's wetland wonders but also to retain them for generations to come.

Great blue heron (*Ardea herodias*) in wetland at day's end.

BIBLIOGRAPHY

Alabama Water Resources Conference. *Proceedings of the 11th Annual Alabama Water Resources Conference, September 3–5, 1997.* Gulf Shores, AL: AWR, 1997.

America's Wetlands: Our Vital Link Between Land and Water. OPA-87-016. Washington: Office of Waterlands Protection, 1988.

Baker, James H. "Wetlands: A Valuable Resource for the '90s." *Pollution Engineering* 25, 8 (April 15, 1993): 38–41.

Blankenship, Donald E., et al. *Key Issues in Wetlands Regulation in Alabama.* Eau Claire, WI: National Business Institute, 1993.

Burke, David G., et al. *Protecting Nontidal Wetlands.* Chicago: American Planning Association, 1988.

Carter, Virginia, and James H. Burbank. *Wetland Classification System for the Tennessee Valley Region.* Norris: Tennessee Valley Authority, 1978.

Commonwealth of Kentucky, Natural Resources and Environmental Protections Cabinet. Draft reports. "Functional Description of Wetland Designated Uses" (January 1993), "Wetland Characterization for Aquatic Life Function" (n.d.), "Proposed Guidance for Wetland Protection and Management in Kentucky (Wetland Biocriteria)" (n.d.), and "Wetland Biocriteria: Selection of Candidate Reference Wetland Sites" (1993). Frankfurt: Commonwealth of Kentucky, Natural Resources and Environmental Protections Cabinet.

Cowardin, Lewis M., et al. *Classification of Wetlands and Deepwater Habitats of the United States.* FWS/OBS-79/31. Washington: US Department of the Interior, 1979.

Dahl, Thomas E., and Craig E. Johnson. *Status and Trends of the Wetlands in the Conterminous United States Mid-1970's to Mid-1980's.* Washington: US Department of the Interior, 1991.

Epperson, Jane E. *Missouri Wetlands: A Vanishing Resource.* Report 39. Rolla: Missouri Department of Natural Resources, Division of Geology and Land Survey, n.d.

"Estuaries." A series of articles in *Oceanus* 19, 5 (Fall 1976): 3–70.

Fisk, David W. (ed.) *Wetlands: Concerns and Successes, Symposium Proceedings, September 17–22, 1989, Tampa, FL.* Bethesda, MD: American Water Resources Association, 1989.

Fretwell, Judy D., John S. Williams, and Phillip J. Redman (comps.) *National Water Summary on Wetland Resources.* Washington: US Geological Survey, 1996.

Frich, Elizabeth, et al. *Water Quality in the Appalachicola–Chattahoochee–Flint River Basin, Georgia, Alabama, and Florida, 1992–1995.* Circular 1164. Washington: US Department of the Interior and US Geological Survey, 1995.

Geological Survey of Alabama. *Shoreline and Bathymetric Changes in the Coastal Area of Alabama: A Remote-Sensing Approach.* Tuscaloosa: Geological Survey of Alabama, University of Alabama, 1975.

Gosselink, James G. *The Ecology of Delta Marshes of Coastal Louisiana: A Community Profile.* FWS/OBS-84/09. Washington: US Department of the Interior, 1984.

Irwin, G. Daniel, and Karen E. Richter. *Alabama Wetlands Land Cover Inventory.* Tuscaloosa: Geological Survey of Alabama, University of Alabama, 1999.

King, Dennis M. "The Economics of Ecological Restoration." Chap. 19 in K. M. Ward and J. W. Duffield (eds.), *Natural Resource Damages: Law and Economics.* New York: John Wiley & Sons, 1992.

Mitsch, William J., and James G. Gosselink. *Wetlands.* 2d ed. New York: Van Nostrand Reinhold, 1993.

National Resources Council. *Wetlands: Characteristics and Boundaries.* Washington: National Resources Council, 1995.

Odum, William E. *The Ecology of Tidal Freshwater Marshes of the United States East Coast: A Community Profile.* FWS/OBS-83/17. Washington: US Department of the Interior, 1984.

Oregon Division of State Lands. *Oregon's Wetland Conservation Strategy.* Salem: Oregon Division of State Lands, 1993.

Protecting Coastal and Wetlands Resources: A Guide for Local Governments. Office of Water (WH-556F), EPA 842-R-92-002. Washington: US Environmental Protection Agency, 1992.

Ransel, Katherine, and Dianne Fish. *Wetlands and 401 Certification: Opportunities and Guidelines for States and Eligible Indian Tribes.* Office of Water (A-104F). Washington: US Environmental Protection Agency, 1989.

Rathburn, Catherine E., et al. *Areal Extent of Wetlands Above and Below the 10-Foot Contour Line in Alabama.* NWRC Open File Report 86-3. Washington: US Department of the Interior, 1987.

Slattery, Britt Eckhardt. *WOW!: The Wonders of Wetlands. An Educator's Guide.* St. Michaels, MD: Environmental Concern, 1991.

Tennessee Wetlands Conservation Strategy. Draft. N.p., n.d.

Urban Wetlands. *Proceedings of the National Wetland Symposium, June 26–29, 1988, Oakland, CA.* Berne, NY: Association of Wetland Managers, 1988.

US Department of the Interior. *America's Endangered Wetlands.* Washington: US Department of the Interior, 1990-259-713.

US Environmental Protection Agency. *Guide to Environmental Issues.* EPA 520/B-94-001. Washington: US Environmental Protection Agency, 1995.

US Environmental Protection Agency. *High Risk Geographic Areas Targeted for Wetlands Advance Identification in Region IV.* Atlanta: Wetlands Planning Unit, US Environmental Protection Agency, 1993.

US Environmental Protection Agency. *Financing State Wetlands Programs.* Washington: US Environmental Protection Agency, Office of Wetlands Protection, 1990.

US Environmental Protection Agency. *The Private Landowner's Wetlands Assistance Guide: Voluntary Options for Wetlands Stewardship in Maryland.* Washington: US Environmental Protection Agency, Wetlands Division, 1992.

US Fish and Wildlife Service. *Mobile River Basin Aquatic Ecosystem Recovery Plan.* Atlanta: US Fish and Wildlife Service, Southeast Region, 1998.

"Vanishing Wetlands." *Reporter* (AAPG Division of Environmental Geosciences) 1, 1 (October 1992).

Wharton, Charles H., Wiley M. Kitchens, and Timothy W. Sipe. *The Ecology of Bottomland Hardwood Swamps of the Southeast: A Community Profile.* FWS/OBS-81/37. Washington: US Department of the Interior, 1982.

World Wildlife Fund. *Statewide Wetlands Strategies: A Guide to Protecting and Managing the Resource.* Washington: Island Press, 1992.

INDEX

National Oceanic and Atmospheric
   Administration (NOAA), 89
National Wild and Scenic River, 10
national wildlife refuge, 11, 87
Native American, 53
natural: events, 56; heritage, vii, 4, 101;
   history, vii, viii, 88; resources, 37, 59, 61,
   90; systems, 51
Nature Conservancy, The, viii, 85, 89
nature preserves, 101
navigation channels, 71
needle rush, 42
nesting grounds, 16
New Jersey, 3
New South, 78
New York, 3
NOAA. *See* National Oceanic and
   Atmospheric Administration
nonattainment site, 79
northern harrier (*Circus cyaneus*), 86
North River, 73
North Temperate Zone, vii
North–South Flyway, 17
nutrients, 38, 39, 40, 42, 43

Oak Mountain State Park, 35, 51
oaks, 74
oasis, 58
Office of Water Resources, 84
officials: local, 98
oil: exploration, 70, 71; production, 71
Old Testament, 58
Omussee Creek, 76
Orange Beach, 20
organizations: private, 85

osprey (*Pandion haliaetus*), 32
oyster reefs, 23
ozone, 78

palustrine, 28. *See also* wetlands: palustrine
paper, 55
parasites, xii
Payne Lake, 90
Perdido Bay, 20, 26, 70
personnel: state regulatory, 98
perspectives: historical, 53
pesticides, 39, 66
Petit Bois Island, 20
petroleum pipelines, 74
photography, xi, xii, 58
physiographic provinces, 8, 18, 73, 75, 76;
   in Alabama, 6; regions, 7
physiography, 7, 28
Piedmont, 8
pitcher plant (*Sarracenia oreophila*), vii, 10, 19
plants: aquatic, 8
pocosins, 28
pollutants, 38, 39, 40, 43; control of, 84;
   gaseous, 78
pollution: control of, 55, 80
ponds, xi, 17, 28, 35, 51, 80; beaver, 52, 60;
   tidal, 29, 39
population, 78; human, 69. *See also*
   growth: population
potholes, 3
Prattville, 73, 74
property: values, 95–96
property rights: groups, 96; private, 95–96
proteins, 43
protozoa, 40

public: activism, 66; involvement, 87
public-use areas, 87

raccoon, 53
rattlebox, 42
reaches: freshwater, 28; shallow water, 28
recreation, 55, 56
recycling, 47; programs, 101
red maple, 19
red-winged blackbird (*Agelaius
   phoeniceus*), 79
refuges: national wildlife, 11, 87; wildlife,
   17, 71
reservoirs, 3, 8, 28, 29
resource managers, 84
Rhode Island, 69
river: bottomlands, 18; commerce, 65;
   deltas, 29
riverfront: improvement, 97
riverine, vii, 28, 65: corridors, 75; systems,
   76. *See also* wetlands: riverine
river otter (*Lutra canadensis*), 48
rivers, viii, 3, 9, 10, 18, 21, 28, 29, 32, 38, 48,
   50, 53, 54, 64, 78, 87, 88; coastal, 28; free-
   flowing, 65; saving, 95; undammed, 75
roadway: construction, 75; infrastructure, 74
Rock Creek, 76
rodents, xi
roosts, 14
roseate spoonbill (*Ajaia ajaja*), 77
runoff, 41, 50, 64
rushes, 42

salamander, viii
salt grass, 43, 46

programs to promote, 88; protection of,
82, 84–86, 90, 94, 95, 101; protection,
challenge of, 98; public appreciation of,
87; regulations, 29, 82, 84; regulatory
provisions, 98; research, 89; resources,
61; riparian, 3; regions, 7; river-bottom,
63; riverine, 28, 29, 32, 76; river-related,
10; roles, 37, 43, 50, 55, 56; scientific
classification, 30; scientific description,
29; settings, 20; shrub, 19; scrub, 30;
southern forested, 55; subsidy
incentives for preserving, 83; sustaining
functions, 37; systematic criteria, 28;
systems, 4, 47, 50, 74, 76, 79, 101; tidal,
20; total area of, 10; types, 7, 28, 29, 30,
32; urban, 3; value of, 37, 61, 62; wild,
19; wild systems, 20

ABOUT THE AUTHOR AND PHOTOGRAPHER

DOUG PHILLIPS is Coordinator for Environmental Information and Education with the Alabama Museum of Natural History. He is also producer of the Public Television series *Discovering Alabama,* an award-winning environmental series that has fostered increased awareness of Alabama's outdoor and natural heritage since the series began in 1985. This video series and its accompanying Teacher's Guides are popular education resources in K–12 classrooms throughout Alabama. A native Alabamian of Creek Indian ancestry, Phillips earned a Ph.D. in Educational Research at The University of Alabama, where he has taught various outdoor courses, including canoeing, orienteering, outdoor survival skills, and environmental education. Among the many educational and research programs he created are "Teaching with Nature: Developing Environmental Education in Alabama Schools" and the Alabama Natural Heritage Program. He is the founding director of the Center for Environmental Research and Service at Troy State University and a founding member of the Alabama Forever Wild Program. Phillips has received numerous awards as a long-standing leader in the environmental field.

ROBERT P. FALLS SR. is a full-time, professional, wildlife and nature photographer, as well as a writer specializing in environmental subjects. His work has been published in books, magazines, calendars, CD-ROM, and on the Internet by such publishers as National Geographic Books, Abbeville Publishing, National Wildlife Federation, Chanticleer Publishing, the Audubon Society, the National Park Service, and others. His work has also been featured in many magazines, including *Outdoor Photographer, Nature Photographer, Outside Magazine, Outdoor Life Magazine,* and *Outdoor Traveler,* and his book, *Exploring Gulf Islands National Seashore,* was published by Globe-Pequot Press in 2001. He is currently the southeastern correspondent for the website Wildlife Watcher.com and a founding member of the Photography Guild of the Birmingham Museum of Art and of the North American Nature Photographers Association. He was commissioned to document homeless people in Birmingham and previously penned monthly columns on photography for the *Birmingham Art Monthly Magazine.* Photographic prints of Falls's work have been added to the collections at museums and corporate offices throughout the Southeast.